The Grover E. Murray Studies in the American Southwest

Also in the series

Agaves, Yuccas, and Their Kin: Seven Genera of the Southwest, by Jon L. Hawker

Brujerías: Stories of Witchcraft and the Supernatural in the American Southwest and Beyond, by Nasario García

Cacti of Texas: A Field Guide, by A. Michael Powell, James F. Weedin, and Shirley A. Powell

Cacti of the Trans-Pecos and Adjacent Areas, by A. Michael Powell and James F. Weedin

Cowboy Park: Steer-Roping Contests on the Border, by John O. Baxter

Dance All Night: Those Other Southwestern Swing Bands, Past and Present, by Jean A. Boyd

Dancin' in Anson: A History of the Texas Cowboys' Christmas Ball, by Paul H. Carlson

Deep Time and the Texas High Plains: History and Geology, by Paul H. Carlson

Finding the Great Western Trail, by Sylvia Gann Mahoney

From Texas to San Diego in 1851: The Overland Journal of Dr. S. W. Woodhouse, Surgeon-Naturalist of the Sitgreaves Expedition, edited by Andrew Wallace and Richard H. Hevly

Grasses of South Texas: A Guide to Identification and Value, by James H. Everitt, D. Lynn Drawe, Christopher R. Little, and Robert I. Lonard

A Kineño's Journey: On Learning, Family, and Public Service, by Lauro F. Cavazos, with Gene B. Preuss

Kit Carson and the First Battle of Adobe Walls: A Tale of Two Journeys, by Alvin R. Lynn

In the Shadow of the Carmens: Afield with a Naturalist in the Northern Mexican Mountains, by Bonnie Reynolds McKinney

Javelinas: Collared Peccaries of the Southwest, by Jane Manaster

Land of Enchantment Wildflowers: A Guide to the Plants of New Mexico, by LaShara J. Nieland and Willa F. Finley

Little Big Bend: Common, Uncommon, and Rare Plants of Big Bend National Park, by Roy Morey

Lone Star Wildflowers: A Guide to Texas Flowering Plants, by LaShara J. Nieland and Willa F. Finley

My Wild Life: A Memoir of Adventures within America's National Parks, by Roland H. Wauer

Myth, Memory, and Massacre: The Pease River Capture of Cynthia Ann Parker, by Paul H. Carlson and Tom Crum

Pecans: The Story in a Nutshell, by Jane Manaster

Picturing a Different West: Vision, Illustration, and the Tradition of Austin and Cather, by Janis P. Stout

Plants of Central Texas Wetlands, by Scott B. Fleenor and Stephen Welton Taber

Seat of Empire: The Embattled Birth of Austin, Texas, by Jeffrey Stuart Kerr

Texas, New Mexico, and the Compromise of 1850: Boundary Dispute and Sectional Crisis, by Mark J. Stegmaier

Texas Quilts and Quilters: A Lone Star Legacy, by Marcia Kaylakie with Janice Whittington

Truly Texas Mexican: A Native Culinary Heritage in Recipes, by Adán Medrano

The Wineslinger Chronicles: Texas on the Vine, by Russell D. Kane

EQUAL OPPORTUNITY HERO

EQUAL OPPORTUNITY HERO

T.J. Patterson's Service to West Texas

Phil Price | Foreword by T.J. Patterson

Texas Tech University Press

Unless otherwise credited, all photographs courtesy of the Patterson family.

This book is typeset in Minion Pro. The paper used in this book meets the minimum requirements of ANSI/NISO Z39.48-1992 (R1997). ♾

Cover photograph courtesy of *Lubbock Avalanche-Journal.*

Cataloging-in-Publication Data is available at the Library of Congress.

17 18 19 20 21 22 23 24 25 / 9 8 7 6 5 4 3 2 1

Texas Tech University Press
Box 41037 | Lubbock, Texas 79409-1037 USA
800.832.4042 | ttup@ttu.edu | www.ttupress.org

Contents

Illustrations

Bringing in the Kindling: A Foreword

Looking back over my life, I am very thankful for having been able to overcome many obstacles that have been in my path. No doubt about it, it has been difficult, but I've made it through by staying focused on what's ahead and believing in the Almighty God.

Perhaps it all began in my life when I was an elementary-school student in Wichita Falls, Texas. I was in the third grade at a school on the grounds of the Booker T. Washington High School. This was during segregation and Jim Crow, and if you were black, well, you couldn't attend a public school where a white student could attend. The elementary classroom at Booker T. Washington High School was not a part of the main three-story building. Therefore, there were always problems in the classroom. During the winter months, there was a heating problem.

Within the classroom, there was a small potbelly stove. In order to be warm during those cold days, the boys of the classroom were organized to bring wood to be burned for heat. The teacher referred to the wood as "kindlin'." Every boy had the responsibility of bringing in kindling.

Not only did we have a responsibility to bring kindling, but the area had to be left in a clean situation. It let us know that we can all make a positive contribution, no matter our station in life. As I look back over my life, I thank God for the opportunity of using kindling for that one aspect, but it did much more.

With resources to keep the entire class warm during the winter months, I thought deeply about that idea. You see, as in life, we need kindling to make things happen. Kindling was a must for me as a young person. No matter the obstacle in my life, I found a way to overcome whatever was in my path.

I remember walking nearly three miles one way to school without being late each morning, regardless of the weather. It taught me a great lesson: never give up, no matter what's in your path. When you were joined with others, it was a great challenge because you knew you could win.

A great challenge in my life came after graduating from high school in 1954. I wanted to attend college, but there were no funds available in my family. During a senior class program, I was awarded a scholarship of $100.00 a year, which was $9.65 a month. It was a work-aid scholarship. I was the janitor for the bathrooms in Marston Hall Dormitory (Men) at Bishop College in Marshall, Texas. This was a very happy moment in my life. This was surely some kindling that served as a catalyst in my life. It was the beginning of many positive things to happen.

"Bringing in the kindling" was necessary for me to move in a positive direction in life. This led me to meet and marry a young lady, Bobbie Gean Bailey in 1960. She was the kindling I needed, as we were married fifty-two and a half years.

T. J. Patterson

Preface

People often preface stories about the past by saying, "Things were different back then." Thomas James (T. J.) Patterson is one man who made those things change. He made a difference by offering ideas and action to settle problems, or as T. J. would say it, he "brought some kindling to the fire."

I've known T. J. for more than twenty years; I have often thought how the respect and friendship I have for him has grown, as has my appreciation for his strength of character, courage, and perseverance. As my research on T. J. began, it quickly showed how growing up black in West Texas was far different from growing up white. Until the research started on this book, I had no idea just how differently T. J. and I had grown up when "things were different back then." T. J. and I grew up during times of great social change that mixed the civil-rights movement of the 1960s with the hippie counterculture's creed of "don't trust anyone over thirty." Both blacks and whites were angry within the diverse movements of that era and wanted drastic change in America, some nonviolently—others far less peacefully.

I witnessed one of the few civil-rights protests staged in Amarillo, Texas, when I was a high-school senior about to graduate in 1961. At noon one day I walked up to Woolworth Variety's lunch counter for a Coke. The store was strangely quiet with little movement by the clerks and clusters of customers. I circled to see what was wrong. In front of me was a well-dressed black guy a little older than I was, sitting alone at the counter with shoebox-size packages on each of the stools and a white string running from one package to another. A Woolworth employee waved me off when I moved toward the counter. My first reaction was, "Why does he need to block the whole counter? I just want one Coke." But then I realized that the civil-rights protests had made it to Amarillo. Suddenly I was in a totally different paradigm than I had awakened to that morning.

The sit-in campaigns of 1960 and the ensuing creation of the Student Nonviolent Coordinating Committee (SNCC) demonstrated the potential strength of grassroots militancy and enabled a new generation of young people to gain confidence in their own leadership. T. J. Patterson went on to make a difference in the attitudes and lives of both blacks and whites in West Texas and beyond during times of drastic change for both races. Those days and years rebuilt the very core of our nation and over time changed how the races looked at each other. It was not an easy transformation, but men and women of both races stepped forward to shape our world for the better.

Throughout my research for this book, I was struck by the lack of information available on black history, especially local and regional information in West Texas. There were the usual tributes to George Washington Carver, Booker T. Washington, and Martin Luther King, Jr., plus famous musicians and sports stars who were often as famous to white America for being black as for their substantial talent that enabled them to succeed—but little else compared to other regions of the United States. West Texas owes much to historians like Paul Carlson, Katie Parks, Eric Strong, Henry Crawford, Daniel Sanchez, Claudia Stuart, and Jean Stuntz for their efforts in bringing much of this hidden history to light. Previously the experiences of black West Texans existed primarily in monographs that identified individuals as "the first black to . . . ," but then failed to drill more deeply.

This book is the attempt to tell part of that fuller story, through the life of one young black man, Thomas James "T. J." Patterson, who along with his friends and family, grew up during that time of social unrest, protest, and upheaval. T. J. Patterson's story is of a man who offered solutions over confrontation and action over rhetoric. His 1984 election to the Lubbock City Council marked a sea of change in Lubbock City Hall. T. J. considered his election not a personal victory but "a victory for us all"—and indeed it was.

EQUAL OPPORTUNITY HERO

Chapter 1

Roads Less Traveled By

On April 7, 1984, T. J. Patterson became the first African American elected to the Lubbock City Council, winning handily over his four opponents in the first regular election that established single-member districts for the city and ended the at-large Lubbock election system adopted in 1917.[1] The change to selecting city representatives finally came after eight long years of court battles, starting on April 1, 1976, when A. Gene Gaines—the first black lawyer to practice in Lubbock—filed a class-action lawsuit on behalf of the black and Hispanic citizens of the city. Representing plaintiff-appellants Reverend Roy Jones, Gonzalo Garza, Antonio Reyes, and intervener Rose Wilson in the lawsuit, Gaines asserted that the system of electing council representatives and the mayor by ballots cast citywide "denies certain classes of people due process" and is therefore unconstitutional.

The suit was filed in the courtroom of US District Judge Halbert O. Woodward, and the trial took place over twelve days, starting on December 11, 1978. At the time approximately 7 percent of the city population was black and 17 percent was Hispanic, with both minority groups concentrated in the east and northeast parts of the city.[2] The plaintiffs' argument was that these minority constituencies had no real access to the political system under an electoral structure that did not acknowledge the geographical isolation of Lubbock minority citizens; the at-large system diluted the voting strength of minority neighborhoods with significant repercussions in municipal maintenance, development, law enforcement, and job opportunities. Decades later, in a 2014 *Avalanche-Journal* retrospective on the change to single-member districts, the current District 1 city councilman, Victor Hernandez, discussed the concentration of representation under the old citywide election system, observing that "if one outlined a quarter on a map of Lubbock, they'd see that every single member lived within that radius."[3] The at-large system had a long history of breeding powerful political cliques in Lubbock, and this class-action suit sought to expand the local leadership pool and provide opportunities for minority representation.

On June 8, 1979, Woodward rendered a judgment in favor of the at-large system. Led by Texas Tech law professor Daniel H. Benson, a team of lawyers including William L. Garrett, Mark C. Hall, Albert Perez, Tomas Garza, and Lane Arthur moved quickly to appeal that decision to the United States Court of Appeals for the Fifth Circuit in New Orleans. They won their challenge, sending the case back to Woodward for reconsideration, with a strong statement from the court of appeals that "the at-large system abridges and dilutes minorities' opportunities to elect members of their own choice." A second trial in Woodward's courtroom took place on January 10–13, 1983. On March 4, 1983, Woodward rendered his decision in favor of the single-member election system and proceeded to divide the city into six councilmember districts, with the mayoral race remaining a citywide election.

The editors of the *Avalanche-Journal* and many other powerful voices were adamantly against the ruling and pushed for an appeal to the United States Supreme Court in defense of the at-large system. As a last stand, on February 16, 1984, the defendants, made up of the sitting city council, sought a stay from the Fifth Circuit. Shortly thereafter, however, the council seemed to recognize the inevitability of the ruling and voted to accept the new single-member system before the court of appeals had rendered a decision on the stay. Under the leadership of the newly elected mayor, Alan Henry, who had taken on the responsibility of the office in a 1983 special election after the tragic death of Mayor Bill McAlister, the presiding council relented in its efforts, and all but Councilman Bud Adderton participated in the April 7, 1984, election through the new district boundaries. Mayor Henry extended an olive branch with his formal announcement of the acceptance of single-member districts, proclaiming that now "minority citizens will not just be supplicants and petitioners but office holders."[4]

Thomas James Patterson was a natural choice to be that trailblazing office holder for the newly constituted single-member District 2. Through his community newspaper, the *Southwest Digest*, Patterson and his partner, Eddie Richardson, had championed the cause of single-member districts at every stage of the court challenge.[5] Patterson and Richardson were experienced journalists and community activists, proudly producing their black-owned and black-operated weekly newspaper to inform and inspire the African American citizens of Lubbock, who lived almost exclusively on the far eastern border of the city in neighborhoods that had been defined by a long and isolating history of forced segregation. These traditional black neighborhoods, clustered together in what is known as the Eastside or East Lubbock, were combined to form single-member city council District 2, and T. J. Patterson was given the chance to expand his already familiar Eastside voice to reach a far broader audience.

Patterson was a talker, full of inspiring words. Richardson was a firebrand, who expressed himself with a blunt edge primarily through his editorial column, "Why Not!" The motto of the newspaper was "Freedom, Justice, and Equality," and the editors wrote and also ran syndicated articles each week on the importance of black empowerment, encouraging black entrepreneurship, celebrating black history, and challenging any form of racial discrimination that occurred on the streets and in the halls of Lubbock institutions. The masthead proclaimed the following: "Devoted to the industrial, education, social, political, and economic advancement of black people."[6]

Started in 1977, the newspaper was originally called the *Lubbock Digest* and quickly became a strong competitor to the existing newspaper serving the Eastside.

Patterson explains the evolution of Eastside news publications: "In about 1968 there was the *Carver Heights News*. James Roy Lewis . . . the black guy ran it. [It] started as the *Carver Heights News* then [he] changed the name of the paper to *Manhattan Heights News* and then the *West Texas Times* when Norman Williamson bought it."

Patterson worked for both owners, serving at various times as advertising director, reporter, and editor. Eddie Richardson also wrote for the *West Texas Times* before partnering with Patterson on their own publication.

Patterson and Richardson met when Patterson was working for Norman Williamson on the *West Texas Times*. Richardson was constantly sending what he terms "hot, hot Letters to the Editor." Then, he says, "T. J. took me out there one Sunday afternoon, and I started writing a regular column."[7]

It wasn't long before Richardson's passion spilled over, and he approached Williamson about a better way to reach out to the black community. Richardson explains the dynamic: "Norman is white and the main reason for why he did the paper, it wasn't as much as he cared about the community; he did it because there was a need for a black newspaper. One day, Norman and I were talking, and I gave him a suggestion on how to run the paper, and Norman told me, 'If you are so damn smart, why don't you start your own paper?' And I said, 'Norman, that's a damn good idea. I think I'll do just that.'"

Patterson gives Richardson full credit for the idea of starting their paper. "It was Eddie's idea," he says. "I didn't want to do it. He wanted to do it. He was very persistent, and he said, 'Let's do something ourselves,' and I kind of hemmed and hawed over it. I didn't want to do it. I didn't want to venture out, so to speak."[8]

Richardson recognized the value of having Patterson in on the publication and tried to be patient. "See, T. J. had the mouth I didn't have," Richardson explains. "He was always out there with the gab. I talked to my partner. 'When are we going to do it?' He said, 'Next week.'"

Richardson grins, "And I figure 'next week' took about three years. . . . After three years, I called him about three or four o'clock in the morning [and] said, 'Man, there isn't going to be no next week. This week: Today. We are going to start our paper, or I am going to start one.' It was a midmorning Wednesday when we started and got through on Thursday morning."

Like Richardson, Patterson remembers that first issue. "We thought that we would never get there, didn't have any equipment. All we had was the IBM machines, some scissors, an old table, a couple glasses, and some glue."

They also had a roll of butcher paper, donated by Richardson's stepfather. It served as a never-ending sheet of typewriter paper, and Richardson adds with a chuckle, "We had a five-dollar bill, and it was my five-dollar bill."[9]

The original headquarters for the *Lubbock Digest* was at 506 East Third Street, just two doors adjacent to what was then a tough bar, the Thunderbird Lounge. The new editors finished that first issue at approximately 1:00 a.m. on Thursday, September 11, 1977. "We had just left," Richardson exclaims, "and this guy got shot dead two doors down that same night."

Patterson remembers the emotions he felt when that first edition rolled off the press. "Bill Loper, a printer at that particular time, printed our first issue, and I couldn't wait to see what it looked like. You thought it would be bigger than it was. You thought you had more pages than you really had, but at the same time, it was impressive. You were tickled to death about it. So it is indescribable. It's like a baby being born."

"We didn't understand what we had done," Patterson adds. "There were so many naysayers that thought we were crazy, that it wouldn't last long, can't make it happen, but all along it was a challenge. There was nothing the like to weigh it against. We had no means of seeing if we were making sense or not, but Reverend A. W. Wilson, he said, 'Regardless what you print, it will be news for black folk in Lubbock, Texas.'"

The deep commitment of Patterson and Richardson to the improvement of the black community underlies the lasting power of the newspaper. On March 18, 1982, they changed the name of the paper to the *Southwest Digest* in recognition of its prominence as a black publication reaching out and responding to the issues of black people throughout the region. Besides a strong emphasis on national, state, and local political issues impacting African Americans, the *Southwest Digest* has also served in many ways as a traditional small-town weekly, publishing obsequies, news about neighborhood schools, club announcements, and reports on community social events.

East Lubbock has a black population of around 9,000[10] and functions very much like a cohesive small town, rooted deeply in church affiliation and attendance. The *Southwest Digest* has always dedicated an entire page to church news each week, with some twenty-eight churches listing their services and activities in the paper. It is primarily through the church page that the paper has performed its valuable outreach services to the surrounding communities, supporting those congregations with announcements of gospel gatherings, guest pastors, and auxiliary meetings. Like black churches throughout the South, the small and intimate congregations of West Texas black churches helped to maintain a sense of community and personal strength through the many blighted years of segregation. They continue their inspirational and aspirational message to this day with an empowering mission and a gospel-music tradition that fills Sunday afternoon on the Eastside with song, oftentimes performed by gospel groups visiting from surrounding towns.

In 1994 Patterson and Richardson moved the newspaper headquarters to 902 East Twenty-eighth Street, setting up shop in the building that once housed the Mary and Mac Private School, owned by Patterson's aunt, Lucille "Sugar" Barton Graves. Today the *Southwest Digest* is still a strong and vibrant newspaper, continuing in its mission to inspire and inform the black citizens of the region. When asked what happened to Williamson and the *West Texas Times*, Patterson echoes Richardson: "Norman continued for a few years and then just faded away."[11]

In 2010, looking back through all the years of weekly publications,

Richardson explains, "The *Southwest Digest* believes . . . we shouldn't wait around for other people to do what we should do ourselves. We've had our ups and downs. We probably been out of business fifteen, twenty times, just didn't close the doors."

Patterson agrees. "We were out of business, didn't know we were out of business, didn't want to quit. We owed rent on 506 Third Street. We'd go out the alleyway to duck her, and she would be waiting for us." Patterson adds his appreciation for their landlady, Ollie Hermanes, who understood what the two activists were attempting to do for their community. "My point I am saying is she knew we were trying . . . long years, tiresome but very rewarding years."

Richardson adds, "The *Southwest Digest*, it's kind of like a ministry. It helped the community quite a bit." And Patterson chimes in, "It tried to do some things that we thought were relevant to the times."[12]

For Patterson and Richardson the seeds of political activism and all those things "relevant to the times" were always deeply rooted in the journalistic "ministry" of the *Southwest Digest*. Patterson took the mission a step farther by combining his talents in journalism with his talents in political leadership, a combination he had begun to cultivate long ago, during his undergraduate years at Bishop College.

In 1954, when Patterson graduated from high school in Wichita Falls, Texas, he was determined to attend college but had very few options available for achieving that goal. His family did not have the means to help him further his education, and at that time, with very few exceptions, Texas colleges and universities were segregated, as were bus stations, public restrooms, drinking fountains, restaurants, most stores, neighborhoods, and just about everything else in the state. Patterson was very grateful to receive a one-hundred-dollar scholarship to Bishop College, a work-aid stipend of $9.65 a month in return for janitorial services.

Bishop College was a black school located in Marshall, Texas, 300 miles east of Wichita Falls. It was founded in 1881 for ex-slaves as part of the ministry of the Baptist Home Mission Society, established by New Yorker Nathan Bishop, who raised $10,000 to start a Texas college for black Baptists.[13] Patterson arrived in the fall of 1954 and embraced college life with a deep commitment to improve himself in every way possible, eagerly supplementing his meager scholarship funds by working odd jobs ranging from washing dishes to shining shoes to just about anything else that would help cover his expenses. For him, the important thing was to make the most of this opportunity to receive a meaningful education.

"I was not a very good student in English," he says, "but I had in mind I would learn how to speak and write the English language." To improve his writing skills, he got involved in the student newspaper, the *Tiger,* and was elected sports director his sophomore year. Covering sports news gave him name recognition, and he soon ventured into campus politics. In his junior year he was elected student body vice president and in his senior year, student body president.

"It was very rewarding being elected as sports director, editor of the *Tiger*, and student body president," Patterson says. "These were all elected positions, which were my first ventures in politics. It was an excellent opportunity for me to grow. It gave me confidence, no matter the obstacles in my path."[14]

The year Patterson became student body president, he ran against his roommate, Virgil Lewis Johnson, who then became student body vice president. The two had become friends in 1954, attending Bishop on the same kind of work-aid stipend. Johnson remembers their college years. Neither of them had any money, but both made the best of their circumstances. Patterson really liked nice clothes, whether they were his or not. Johnson and his classmates shared a running joke that "every time one of us had a date, we had to undress T. J. to get our clothes back." Johnson expands on their sharing: "If I didn't go to church, and T. J. wanted to go to church, well, he would borrow some of my clothes and wear them and bring them back, and I would get some of his. Well, it wasn't just T. J. and Virgil; it was some other guys around there, too."[15]

Elijah Donaldson, a childhood friend of Patterson and a Bishop student for part of the time that Patterson and Johnson were at the college, remembers why Patterson might have enjoyed borrowing Johnson's clothes. "I met him when I went to Bishop," says Donaldson. "Virgil was the sharpest dressed on the Bishop campus, and he always was singing."[16]

Both Patterson and Johnson graduated in 1958, Patterson in May and Johnson in August. After graduation Johnson secured a position teaching English at Blackshear, the African-American high school in Odessa, Texas, and soon found a public forum for his singing. By the next school year he had talked four of his students into joining him in forming a quintet. The group performed at school dances, with Johnson as lead tenor, and created their own very polished style of doo-wop music. Rising West Texas rock-and-roll star Roy Orbison heard them perform on a visit to

Odessa and recommended them to his producer, Fred Foster of Monument Records. Foster gave them the name "the Velvets featuring Virgil Johnson," and they recorded a 1961 hit "Tonight (Could Be the Night)," written by Johnson. It peaked on the charts at number twenty-six. Their second single, "Lana," co-written by Roy Orbison and Joe Melson, reached number one in Japan. Monument ultimately recorded nine singles by the group, but their smooth, melodious sound, often accompanied by strings, didn't quite fit into the pop-music categories of the time, and by 1966 Johnson had returned to West Texas and his teaching career. Nevertheless, the Velvets remain a celebrated doo-wop group to this day, and their complete recorded output of thirty songs was collected on compact disc and released on Ace Records in 1996.[17]

Johnson's musical success did not surprise Patterson. He remembers that during their college years Johnson was always practicing his singing. When asked why he didn't join in, Patterson admits, "I wasn't good at singing. They wouldn't let me sing with 'em. Virgil was good though. They practiced all night long."

According to Johnson, singing wasn't the only thing his roommate couldn't do well. Johnson chuckles, remembering Patterson's performance on the basketball court. "T. J. went out for the basketball team. He couldn't play a lick, but whenever T. J. hit the court, the stands went wild."

Johnson explains that when Patterson raced downcourt and shot the ball, he seemed to always wind up running up into the stands, and the fans roared, whether he scored or not. Johnson laughs and adds, "They went wild. He tried to contribute to the team, and he did, but he still couldn't play."

Johnson remembers another event at Bishop College that makes him laugh. It began one Sunday morning when Johnson and Patterson decided to skip the mandatory church services. Johnson and another student were "rolling the bones" in what must have been a very low-stakes dice game.

"At Bishop College," Johnson explains, "every Sunday you must go to chapel . . . or you must go to church. T. J. Patterson, Bob King, and I were up there playing cards, and the windows were open. The campus is very small, and we were getting loud. . . . Now, T. J. was not playing; he was in bed.

"We heard a knock at the door. Bob King says, 'Grease your belly and slide under the door.' There was another knock. Bob says again, 'I said, grease your belly and slide under,' and the door opens. It was the president of the college, Dr. Milton K. Curry. T. J. yanked the covers over his head and just laid still. He didn't move."

In retrospect, Johnson recalls the scene as much funnier than it probably felt at the time. "That was the funniest thing," Johnson insists. "I tell you what, the fact that T. J. was there saved our hides, because T. J.'s auntie, Miss Graves, knew President Curry, and they were close. That is why we were at Bishop, and that's why we graduated."[18]

Patterson's aunt, Sugar Graves, was a strong role model and guide for both these young men. She received her bachelor's degree in education from Butler College in Tyler, Texas, and married and moved to Lubbock in 1952. In 1955 Graves established the Mary and Mac Private School in East Lubbock, naming the school after the children's nursery rhyme that, she explains, "depicts the act of boys and girls in their desire to become useful in this society."[19]

It is not surprising that Graves knew Bishop College President Dr. Milton K. Curry. The network of black educators in segregated Texas ran deep and wide, and Curry had great ambitions for his school. He became president of Bishop College in 1952 and quickly began to develop funds to move the school from the small town of Marshall to Dallas, with the goal of expanding enrollment, course offerings, and degree programs to make Bishop College a nationally known premier black college. Dallas was the only city in the nation with a significant black population that did not have a black college, and in 1956, with representatives from the United Negro College Fund, Curry was able to make that argument to a large group of Dallas millionaires, successfully generating most of the funding to secure the land and build the campus for a Bishop College relocation to Dallas. In an article published in *Magazine* in 1987, Curry admits that many of these wealthy city leaders were probably more interested in maintaining segregation than furthering black education. "I think," he says, "they felt we eventually were going to arrive in Dallas anyway, so they'd be better off seeing to it that Bishop's arrival was more comfortable for them, and not to us. It really didn't matter then, because I figured it to be that way."[20]

Plans proceeded for the relocation of the school to take place in 1961. Patterson's four years at Bishop College, from 1954 to 1958, were the final few of that school in Marshall, Texas, placing him on the cusp of a new era for his alma mater and, as it happened, a new era for black education throughout the nation. His freshman year saw the 1954 landmark US Supreme Court decision of *Brown v. Board of Education*, which opened the pathway to an organized struggle for racial equality and the dramatic beginnings of the civil-rights movement.

In *Brown v. Board of Education* the Supreme Court ruled that the concept of "separate but equal" in public education was unconstitutional. To all who had eyes, it was obvious that racially separating students by school was never equal. Many black schools didn't even have enough textbooks for the students, let alone the physical space to accommodate the student population. The unanimous ruling by the US Supreme Court mandated desegregation of public schools nationwide, and the process proved to be a wrenching affair, not just in the southern states but also throughout the nation, where neighborhoods and areas of town had traditionally determined public-school attendance.

Many efforts to maintain the status quo brought about loud and overt defiance of the ruling, most notably in Little Rock, Arkansas, where in 1957 President Dwight D. Eisenhower had to call out the 101st Airborne Division and federalize the Arkansas National Guard in order to protect the black students enrolling in Little Rock Central High School. Opposition to the ruling also led to quieter and, in some ways, more insidious tactics, like establishing private white schools funded with public monies. One way or another, somewhere or another, the desegregation process has remained in the courts since the *Brown* decision. Nevertheless, the ruling profoundly, if gradually, shifted the habits and thinking of the nation, and with the legal system finally looking over them—at least at the federal level—black citizens were filled with a new hope and confidence that they could actually eliminate segregation as a legal institution. What had been an authoritarian system of white dominance under decades of Jim Crow laws became a significant clash of cultural values that changed the very fabric of the nation.

Certainly the old ways in the South continued at many levels. At the beginning of Patterson's sophomore year, on August 28, 1955, Emmett Till, a fourteen-year-old Chicago African American, who was visiting relatives in Mississippi, was kidnapped, beaten, killed, and dumped in the Tallahatchie River for making an overture to a white woman. Some say he whistled at her. Some say he spoke to her in a cocky, flirty way. All say he was killed for his behavior.[21] The Tuskegee Institute has maintained a statistical listing of lynchings in the United States since 1892, and the record notes that between 1882 and 1951, 4,730 people were lynched. Of those, nine-tenths were lynched in the South and 3,437 of them were African American, often for committing social improprieties.[22] Traditionally, this form of vigilante justice gained little public notice outside of perhaps a note in the local newspaper, but the killing of Emmett Till generated national attention and became a touchstone for the nascent civil-rights movement.

In that same year, on December 1, 1955, Rosa Parks refused to give up her city bus seat to a white man in Montgomery, Alabama, and was arrested for her defiance. The press had become interested in the ways of the segregated South, and this incident, while not the first of its kind, became a national news story and another touchstone for the civil-rights movement, precipitating the Montgomery bus boycott. The boycott lasted a year, virtually bringing the city bus lines to a standstill, and only came to an end through another Supreme Court ruling that mandated the desegregation of city bus lines.[23]

As the president of the Montgomery Improvement Association (MIA), the Reverend Martin Luther King, Jr., led the protest and inspired the participants with his message of freedom delivered in the thunderous tones of his own style of revival rhetoric. With the grassroots expertise of Ella Baker, King mobilized the black community to boycott the buses and coordinated the complicated logistics of the prolonged demonstration. People with cars took turns giving rides to those who needed to go to work, go home, pick up children, buy groceries, or visit sick relatives, providing the transportation necessary to ensure that people could function in their lives while the protest proceeded. This grueling but successful boycott established the organizational model for nonviolent protests to come. Sit-ins and challenges to interstate transportation, the right to vote, voter registration, and media relations were all coordinated protest efforts to destroy Jim Crow laws by challenging them in court and shining a harsh light on the old ways in order to reveal them as the barbaric system they had always been.[24]

In 1955 Patterson was a nineteen-year-old observer of the scene, living in the cloistered environment of Bishop College as the outside world spun wildly and, for the first time since Reconstruction, in his people's direction. The fight for equal justice was dangerous, and was primarily being played out most overtly and violently in Alabama and Mississippi. During his years at Bishop College, there were no public actions by African Americans to disrupt the segregated status quo in Marshall, Texas. As Patterson explains, "Marshall was a small city with a large population of Negros or 'Colored' people. This gave me an idea of problems in Marshall." Patterson's time in college was too early in the movement for people on the periphery to muster the organizational resources for meaningful action, and Patterson did not consider using his elected position as sports editor of the *Tiger* to promote civil rights, even though there were certainly many meaningful examples of racial discrimination in the athletic arena.

He explains, “Despite the black population of Waxahachie and Marshall being larger than the white, the black students and adults feared the repercussions of the white population that controlled the positions of power.”[25]

Of course, that intimidation of a large black population by a white power structure was characteristic of circumstances throughout the Old South and the elemental reason for the blanket subjugation policies of Jim Crow put in place after Reconstruction. White Southerners feared the influence of a black population that could receive a meaningful education, compete for good jobs, and elect black representatives. They could not understand a world beyond racial identity and were tribal and violent in their efforts to maintain their position of supreme privilege and power. Patterson often muses about his attitudes growing up and how easily he accepted the dictates of segregation, admitting that he, like virtually every other black person in the nation outside of Harlem, just assumed, as he says, that “that's just the way things were.”

By 1957 the way things were had definitely begun to change. The legal and activist rumblings in the Deep South emanating from *Brown v. Board of Education* and the Montgomery bus boycott led to a mighty civil-rights coalition, often called the “Big Four”: the SCLC, the NAACP, CORE, and SNCC. The SCLC (Southern Christian Leadership Conference) was founded in 1957 under the leadership of Martin Luther King, Jr., and Ralph Abernathy. The SCLC organized civil-rights groups primarily through church affiliations. The venerable NAACP (National Association for the Advancement of Colored People), under the leadership of Roy Wilkins, served as the legal arm of the movement, sending a phalanx of eminent black lawyers, like Thurgood Marshall, to argue before the US Supreme Court, one case after another. Established in 1942 by James L. Farmer, Jr., CORE (Congress of Racial Equality) turned its focus away from its Chicago base to join the struggle of ending segregation in the Deep South. CORE had years of experience organizing sit-ins and jail-ins in the upper Midwest and, among many other things, used its well-established, interracial network to recruit idealistic young people from outside the South to participate in the Freedom Rides of 1961. With ever-growing enthusiasm, students, both black and white, were responding to the cause, and in 1960 Ella Baker founded SNCC (Student Nonviolent Coordinating Committee) to serve as a crucial ground operation for the movement. The grassroots organizing expertise of Ella Baker served as the underpinning for coalition resistance strategies throughout the struggle, and together these four organizations coordinated a nonviolent protest campaign that changed the sensibilities of and possibilities for black citizens throughout the nation.[26]

One year after Patterson graduated, in 1959, President Curry invited Reverend Martin Luther King, Jr., to be the commencement speaker at Bishop College, helping to bring the little school into the vibrant spirit of the times. Bishop alumnus Dr. Harry Blake attended that commencement ceremony and was inspired enough to travel to Atlanta, Georgia, to meet with Reverend Ralph Abernathy and Dr. King. Blake was made SCLC field secretary for Shreveport, Louisiana, just forty miles east of Marshall. Early in 1960 he contacted Dr. Doxey Wilkerson, a new Bishop faculty member, just arrived from New York City. Blake convinced Wilkerson to help organize a sit-in at the segregated Marshall Woolworth lunch counter. This was just two months after the first lunch counter sit-in in Greensboro, North Carolina, an organized student nonviolent protest that marked the beginning of student activism in the struggle.

Throughout the Jim Crow era, Texas showed itself to be a tried-and-true daughter of the Confederacy. From 1900 to 1910, Texas lynched around a hundred black men, sometimes including ritualized torture in the process. Texas was also one of six states still supporting a whites-only primary election until it was declared illegal by the US Supreme Court in 1944. While Texas was never a central battleground for the civil-rights movement and boasted an active and decidedly progressive wing of the then one-and-only Democratic party, Texas laws and cultural traditions were steeped in the ways of the slave-holding South. In 1956 Governor R. Allan Shivers adamantly opposed *Brown v. Board of Education* and sent the Texas Rangers to Mansfield, Texas, to prevent black students from integrating the public high school. Texas required a poll tax in all elections until the Twenty-fourth Amendment, passed in 1964, eliminated the practice for federal elections. In 1966 the US Supreme Court ruled the poll tax unconstitutional in state elections as well.[27]

Patterson's caution concerning Marshall, Texas, was certainly well placed. The town was founded in 1841, and by the beginning of the Civil War, it was the fourth-largest city in Texas, with more slaves than any other place in the state. Marshall is located just twenty-two miles from Caddo Lake, a natural wetland split between Texas and Louisiana, which features bayous, alligators, and cypress trees draped with moss. This is definitely the environment of East Texas, far different from the West Texas rangeland and ranch culture of Patterson's home in Wichita Falls, a classic frontier town incorporated in 1889, long after emancipation. By contrast, Marshall played a significant role in the Civil War as a production center and the western capital of the Confederacy.

During Reconstruction the town had an office of the Freedmen's Bureau and was a base for Union troops. Many freed slaves came to Marshall, and in reaction an insurgent militia rose up to advocate for and defend white supremacy. Inspired by the number of ex-slaves residing in Marshall, two different Christian denominations established black colleges in the town as part of their missionary program. Bishop College was founded to educate freedmen and bring them into the Baptist faith. Earlier, in 1873, Wiley College was founded in Marshall by the Methodist Episcopal Church to educate ex-slaves and help further a distinctly American form of Methodism. In 1960 the two colleges together served approximately 900 students in this small, East Texas town of 25,000 residents.[28]

Bill Moyers won a Primetime Emmy in 1984 for his PBS documentary "Marshall, Texas: Marshall, Texas," a title based on the white-and-black racial divide in the town. In the film Moyers interviews the townspeople and shares his memories of growing up in Marshall during the 1940s and early 1950s. He also investigates the nature of the "two towns" that characterized Marshall under the strict tenets of segregation. As Patterson says about his student years in Marshall, "We didn't go downtown much."[29] Moyers includes an interview with longtime CORE director James L. Farmer, who was also born and raised in Marshall. Farmer received his bachelor's degree at Wiley College before leaving for graduate school at Howard University School of Religion. Both Moyers and Farmer pay tribute to their upbringing in the little town, but Farmer makes it clear that his early commitment to racial equality stems from the deep racial divide he experienced growing up in Marshall, Texas. In 1960 the social activism that shaped Farmer's adult life finally reached his hometown and his alma mater.[30]

Besides Dr. Doxey Wilkerson from Bishop College, Blake contacted Dr. Cuthbert Simpkins at Wiley College to help coordinate the Woolworth sit-in. Students from both colleges were trained in the tenets of nonviolent protest, and the ensuing sit-in lasted from March 26 to April 3, 1960. It all began when a combination of ten black students from both Bishop and Wiley walked into the local Woolworth and sat down at the whites-only lunch counter, requesting service. The store manager immediately turned off the lights and closed the lunch counter. The protest quickly gained momentum and was officially named the Wiley-Bishop Student Movement, with students occupying seats at the Woolworth lunch counter, the Union bus terminal cafe, and the Fry-Hodges Rexall Drug lunch counter. With each effort the counters were closed. On March 30, for their attempts to be served, fifty-seven students were arrested and jailed by order of Harrison County District Attorney Allen for unlawful assembly under Article 439 of the Texas Penal Code, originally established to combat strikes. Around 600 other students gathered at the courthouse to support the protesters. The white reaction to the sit-in followed what would become a familiar pattern.

Under the authority of county and city leaders, the fire department was called in to disperse the students, entering the scene with four fire trucks and three hoses and dousing the protesters with stronger and stronger blows of water. Local law enforcement also sent for the Texas Rangers, highway patrolmen, and police officers from neighboring towns to keep the peace between hundreds of roaming students and white agitators parading German shepherd and Doberman attack dogs around the town square.[31]

By March 31 the Wiley-Bishop sit-in had caught the attention of the media, with reporters from the *Texas Observer*, the *Dallas Morning News*, the *Dallas Times Herald*, the *Shreveport Times*, and the *Associated Press* descending on Marshall. The sit-in was also being monitored by the *London Times* through telephone calls. The media was greeted with universal hostility from the white townspeople and the local newspaper and radio station. In fact, the owner of the local radio station refused to aid the reporters with any of his media resources, and the *Marshall New Messenger* and business leaders agreed to limit coverage of the demonstrations to diminish interest. Of course, these attempts at a news blackout failed.

Patterson heard about the protest from friends he still had at Bishop College and was amazed it had happened in Marshall. He was also filled with admiration for "the brave folk to stand up to what was right" and a deep conviction that "it was about time!"[32] In his interview with Bill Moyers, James Farmer talks about the student movement, noting, "I cannot tell you how pleased I was when I picked up the *New York Times* one morning and saw that Wiley College students were a part of it. They too were marching. That made me weep; it brought me to tears."[33]

The students continued their protest until April 3, with many arrested and local African American leaders providing bail since bond was set through property. The sit-in had caused a 50 percent decline in local business, and the townspeople made a passionate appeal to both college presidents to bring about a cessation to the demonstration. On April 1 Presidents Curry and Cole responded by calling for an end to the protest, but both refused to dismiss the sit-in as a fad and complimented the students on their goals. The Bishop students agreed to end the demonstration. Wiley students continued for one more day but with waning support and enthusiasm. On Sunday, April 3, 1960, the Wiley-Bishop Student Movement officially came to an end, and court actions followed. Local judges found fifty-seven students guilty of unlawful assembly, six for unlawful picketing, and sixteen for failing to vacate, but the students were vindicated on appeal when the Texas Court of Criminal Appeals rendered the unlawful assembly law too vague to apply to the circumstances—or by implication, any other circumstances. Nevertheless, court actions continued until December of 1962.[34]

Curry succeeded in moving Bishop College to Dallas as planned in 1961 and more than doubled its enrollment, faculty, and degree programs in the next decade. In 1975 he became president of the United Negro College Fund during the heyday of that organization's most famous public campaign, advertising for scholarship support with the famous phrase coined by Young & Rubicam, "A Mind is a Terrible Thing to Waste."[35]

While Bill Moyer's documentary is, in many ways, a nostalgia piece on small-town living, with a particular lament for the racial divide that characterized the history of Marshall, it is also a celebration of the changes that have taken place. The Marshall public-school system was integrated in 1964. By 1984 the very year that single-member representation came to Lubbock, Moyer's film reveals that the town had embraced a black postmaster, black clerks in banks, black saleswomen in stores, a black mayor, a black county commissioner, and a black physician elected president of the local medical association.[36]

The Wiley-Bishop sit-in, its trained and disciplined student protestors, the aggressive reaction of law enforcement, and the legal aftermath that gave shape to the injustice, were elements that had just begun to form a predictable pattern in 1960. Just two years earlier, when Patterson graduated from his beloved Bishop College, campus civil-rights protests were still an unimagined phenomenon. In 1958 the civil-rights movement was primarily focused on desegregation court cases and on fine-tuning the organizational structure that would soon test the engrained tenants of

Plessey v. Ferguson in the field, calling the question on "separate but equal" into every corner of American life. It had not yet mobilized the student resources it would need for an organized ground game.[37] Patterson left Bishop College with the standard goals of a 1950s college graduate—to get a good job and better his personal circumstances.

Graduating with a degree in marketing, he returned home to Wichita Falls to assess his options and was soon offered a position in Fort Worth, selling whole-life insurance in a portion of the city called the "Boneyard" by his employer. The insurance company required agents to collect the weekly premiums with an 80 percent collection rate. It was a challenging job, but Patterson was determined to succeed. A favorite cousin, Oma Love Cleaver, had given him a briefcase as a graduation present. He arrived in Fort Worth with his very professional briefcase, a few clothes, a YMCA membership, and eight dollars in his pocket.

As a member of the YMCA, Patterson could stay at the "Y" for six dollars a week and have two dollars to live on. In those days employees often kept money "in the hole," retaining funds that had been earned but were not distributed until payday, one or two weeks away. Those who quit early forfeited their money "in the hole." These were challenging days for the new graduate, but he persevered.

Every morning Patterson got up and walked to his job site in downtown Fort Worth. He recalls that it was on Missouri Street by the old Kent Cadillac Company. Before he walked the distance, he would try to find something to fill his empty stomach. He remembers his morning breakfast in those early days: "I would get up. There was a black sister had a restaurant. As I raised out my window I could smell her grits and eggs. I would just smell and say, 'Lord help me,' and I would just smell and get full, have a drink of water, then walk to work."

This was his lean regimen for about a month, until an old man noticed what he was doing and made him an offer of room and board for twenty-five dollars a week, proposing, "We'll let you stay with us, and we'll feed you, and for an extra ten dollars, we'll wash your clothes."

Patterson jumped at the offer and remembers it with words of praise, "Lord have mercy, that's a blessing!" Even though he was without a car, he now had a place to sleep and food to eat. He felt like a real insurance agent.

Some might have had second thoughts about a territory that lay on the rough south side of Fort Worth, but Patterson rejoiced at having an occupation, even if it was in a section of town that had been dominated by stockyard slaughterhouses for decades, a history that had earned it the moniker of the "Boneyard," from the cattle bone remains of Armour, Swift and Company, and other meat-packing operations. In the late 1950s, after a half century of dominating the industry, the Fort Worth stockyards were falling into decline.[38]

Swift and Company and Armour were enticed to join in a meat-packing venture with businessman, Greenlief W. Simpson, a wealthy Bostonian who had moved to Fort Worth in 1893. Simpson sought to establish a gathering point for regional livestock by offering Texas cattlemen fifty cents more for each head than the livestock market in Kansas City. The agreement was finalized in 1902, and Swift and Company opened in March of 1904, followed quickly by Armour.

This arrangement created an efficient method for supplying the nation with beef and other meat products, and for decades the conglomerate of Fort Worth meatpackers and Texas cattlemen shared a very profitable operation, but in 1921 Congress passed the Packers and Stockyards Act to limit the influence of meatpackers who held a virtual monopoly on the industry. This act required meatpacking companies to liquidate their interests in the ancillary businesses of stockyards, banks, cattle loan companies, railroads, and industry trade publications. Through litigation, Swift and Armour were able to stave off compliance for over a decade, but divestiture finally arrived, accompanied by the droughts and financial disasters of the Great Depression. Unions and technological advances further decentralized the industry. By the 1950s Swift and Amour were at the tag end of their Fort Worth operations. Armour closed its Fort Worth plant in 1962, followed by Swift in 1971.[39]

Patterson's territory was a dying part of town. He describes it as a terrible place; nevertheless, it was his place. Every morning he would make his way to the slowly crumbling area by catching the bus to Stop Six, then catching another bus to Lake Como before getting off at the Boneyard. He worked every inch of the place, and although he didn't have a car, he was never mugged and was always on time and ready to go. He got up early, worked late, and then finally resolved to look for another opportunity. The dearth of potential clients in the Boneyard, plus the payout policies of the insurance company, just made it impossible for him to make any money. He thought he had found a promising opportunity when he applied at the Fort Worth Bethlehem Recreational Center, but the center chose another applicant.[40] Fortunately, the disappointment at not getting the job was soon soothed by an offer from Patterson's Aunt Lucille Graves, the seventeenth child of his grandmother and the older sister of his mother, who was the eighteenth child of his grandmother.

Graves offered Patterson a car, a 1951 Plymouth stick shift, as a graduation present if he would come to Lubbock and pick it up. As he trudged the Boneyard and even as he anticipated the possibility of working at the Bethlehem Recreational Center, Patterson was formulating a long-term plan to join Martin Luther King in the great struggle for equal rights. This car was just what he needed to get him to Atlanta, Georgia. Patterson borrowed a little money, quit his job, and headed for Lubbock on a TNM&O bus to pick up his car and head for the epicenter of the civil-rights movement. He remembers, "I was going to Atlanta, Georgia, my brother. I was going to work my way all the way to Georgia, washing dishes, anything, to get there."

On August 29, 1958, Patterson arrived in Lubbock, then a small city of around 100,000 inhabitants and, besides family, the hometown of his old roommate, Virgil Johnson. Patterson says Johnson was always trying to get him to move to Lubbock, and here he finally was, at least for a rest stop before taking to the road on his grand adventure. Patterson called his Aunt April Rose from the "colored" section of the bus station to pick him up and take him to the home of his Aunt Lucille. She told him to just take a cab, and he was stunned at the extravagance, explaining to her that he had no money. But to this aunt, cab fare was nothing. She repeated, "You catch a cab."

Patterson explains, "That aunt . . . was a bootlegger . . . a tough lady. Ironically, it was often the bootleggers who were first to financially support the churches and their building efforts. In those days, bootlegging was a generally accepted means of skirting liquor laws. Later many of the bootleggers opened cafes and clubs in Lubbock when things were different."

What Patterson saw of Lubbock was the Eastside, and he was definitely not impressed. East Lubbock was a conspicuously neglected and racially isolated area of this thriving and ever-growing city, and his first impressions strengthened his resolve to join Dr. King in Atlanta as soon as possible. However, his Aunt Lucille was convinced that he should stay in Lubbock, and she upped the ante by offering him a job teaching high school at the Mary and Mac Private School. He decided to work there long enough to earn the money he needed to join Dr. King in the cause. Patterson soon found out, however, that he loved teaching, and he gradually settled into the rhythm of the classroom and the community. The trip to Lubbock to pick up that old used car proved to be the seminal turning point in T. J. Patterson's life.[41]

Chapter 2

Family Matters

It didn't take long for Patterson to expand his involvement in the Mary and Mac School. Besides teaching English courses at the newly established high school, he volunteered as a baseball coach and drove the school bus. With his earnings, Patterson soon traded in that 1951 Plymouth for a red convertible and began to envision a meaningful future through his work in East Lubbock. That future gained a new impetus when Patterson saw a picture of Bobbie Gean Bailey in a 1959 newspaper edition of *Kansas City: The Call*. The beautiful Miss Bailey, who hailed from Lubbock, had just graduated magna cum laude from Paul Quinn College in Waco, Texas, and a Waco stringer for the *Call* had shot the photograph of her that ran in the paper.[1]

People on the Eastside saw that picture and were proud to have a young member of the Lubbock community in such a distinguished publication. At the time, the *Call* was one of the top six African American weeklies in the nation. Longtime NAACP director Roy Wilkins was a reporter and managing editor of the *Call* from 1923 to 1931, right after he graduated from the University of Minnesota and just before he joined the NAACP to soon become the editor of the *Crisis*. The *Call* served black communities throughout the region with news affecting African Americans and strong editorials written from a black perspective and celebrating black achievements, encouraging black businesses, and voicing black concerns.

Founded in 1919 by Chester A. Franklin, the *Call*, along with many other African American newspapers all over the nation, served the interests of black people during the long and isolating era of segregation. When the achievements of the civil-rights movement gained influence over coverage of black issues in the mainstream press, many African American newspapers folded. The *Call* was an exception and continued weekly publication well into the twenty-first century for the black communities of Kansas City, Kansas, and Kansas City, Missouri. In 1959 the paper was a significant regional news source and had many readers in Lubbock, including T. J. Patterson, whose own publication years later would share a similar philosophy and format as the *Call*.[2]

Patterson was swept away by that photograph of Bobbie Gean Bailey and thrilled to realize that she lived in Lubbock. Bobbie had just won a beauty contest at the Mae Simmons Park swimming pool, and Patterson immediately began to devise a strategy for wooing her. He says of his plans, "When I saw her, I knew I had to have her, and I went and got her."

As it happened, Patterson was coaching Bobbie's sister on the Mary and Mac baseball team, and Bobbie remembers their first meeting. "My sister and a friend of mine was playing baseball. T. J. was the coach. . . . I was trying out for the softball team and that was the first time I met him."

Her first impression was of his car more than his coaching or his looks. "Well," she says, "going by what they told me, he had a brand new 1959 red Plymouth Fury convertible with a continental kit on the back, and I thought he had some money. Come to find out, he didn't, but I knew his Aunt April real well 'cause she was a friend of my grandmother's."

Bobbie didn't seem to share Patterson's instant infatuation. In fact, she had multiple beaux vying for her favor. "I was pretty popular," she says. "I had a couple boyfriends down there in college . . . so, you know, I wasn't hurtin'." She goes on: "I had one boyfriend that my mother didn't like. . . . The one that I liked, they didn't like him. T. J. was nice. He'd drive by every day or stop to speak to my grandmother. So he won them over. . . . I had to let two or three other friends go . . . and, in fact, there was a boy in college I was engaged to that I let go."[3]

Driving the Mary and Mac school bus was a boon to Patterson's courtship. Bobbie's baby brother, Hillary Hutchinson, rode the bus, and as little Hillary got off at his home, Patterson would pinch his cheek, just enough to make him cry, then tell him to call for his big sister to come get him. Bobbie came out the first time to soothe her crying brother, but soon she was greeting the bus in her own interests.

The Bethel African Methodist Episcopal Church was another place Patterson knew he could be with Bobbie. The Bethel AME Church was a very important part of her life. A church that holds the distinction of being "the oldest independent Protestant denomination founded by black people in the world," the AME Church was founded in 1816 as an African

American congregation to be independent from the racial discrimination of white Methodists in Philadelphia, Pennsylvania. During Reconstruction the denomination grew exponentially in the South. By the turn of the twentieth century, it had hundreds of thousands of members and operated over 2,000 black schools, among them Paul Quinn College, where Bobbie attended through support from her hometown congregation. She explains, "They have to send the money anyway, so the money they sent would be used to support me and my sister. We got some aid from our church to go to school. I graduated with a bachelor's degree in elementary education. Later, I got a master's degree from Texas Tech."[4]

In that summer of 1959, Sundays found Patterson joining the congregation at Bethel AME Church, and the pastor was fully aware that the young man's quest was not totally spiritual. He warned Patterson about poaching off his flock and told Bobbie, "If he can come to church to visit, he can join." She adds, "Everybody liked T. J. because he was really easygoing, and he was a nice person. Everybody in town liked him."

Thomas James Patterson and Bobbie Gean Bailey were married on August 19, 1960, in the Bethel AME Church, where Patterson had become a member and proceeded to be a devoted and active participant in church worship and activities from that time on. College roommate and dear friend Virgil Johnson served as their best man and, with help from Curtis Gibson and Virgil Smith, may very well have caused the couple's first tiff.

When the newlyweds dashed from the church to Patterson's new convertible, they discovered that someone had drained all the gas from the tank. Sitting in that stalled car, they had their first argument, no doubt over Patterson's buddies and their silly sense of humor. T. J. always chuckled about the incident; Bobbie, not so much, but the disagreement didn't run very deep, and the young couple had many things in common to help them build a strong relationship and marriage.

Besides being dedicated educators, they were both raised in similar families, with devoted, hard-working mothers and grandmothers who lent emotional support to their daughters and grandchildren. They were also both fortunate to be raised by committed and loving stepfathers. Neither had much awareness or early contact with their biological fathers.

Bobbie was raised in Lubbock. "My family came to Lubbock in the 1930s," she says, "and, actually, I was born out here with another sister . . . who was a year younger than me. . . . My granddaddy had what they called a juke joint, and we lived in the area known as 'the Flats.'"[5] The Flats was the original area of town cordoned off for black people, stretching from

Nineteenth Street to Sixteenth Street and from Avenue A to Avenue C. This section of town had been defined in 1923 by an ordinance proposed to the Lubbock city council. The ordinance reads:

> *Within which Negroes and persons of African descent, containing as much as one-eighth Negro blood, shall reside, except bona fide servants residing on the place where employed. Forbidding persons to sell property outside of such district to Negroes or persons containing as much as one-eighth Negro blood. Forbidding the rental of property outside such district. Providing penalties and declaring an emergency account of Negroes living in other districts and causing danger to health and pollution of the atmosphere. Be it ordained by City Council (Commission) of the City of Lubbock, Texas.*
>
> *Section I—No Negro or person of African descent or containing as much as one-eighth Negro blood shall own property or reside thereon in any part of the City, except that part lying south of 16th Street and east of Avenue C and no person shall rent or lease to any such Negro or persons of African descent or one containing as much as one-eighth Negro blood, outside of the territory limits as above.*
>
> *Section II—Section I shall not apply to bona fide servants living on the premises of their employer. Provided that such servant or servants shall receive living quarters as part of their compensation and that such servants shall be employed the major portion of their time by the family or persons on whose premises they reside.*
>
> *Section III—Any person violating any part of this ordinance shall, upon conviction, be punished by fine of not more than two hundred dollars and each transaction or day's residence shall constitute a separate offense.*
>
> *Section IV—The fact that Negroes and persons of African descent and persons containing as much as one-eighth Negro blood are residing in various portions of this City and their residence is dangerous to the health and pollutes the earth and atmosphere, creates an emergency and necessity that the removal of the Charter requiring an ordinance to be read at two meetings be suspended and this ordinance be enacted at the meeting of its introduction and effective upon publication.*[6]

While there is no evidence that this ordinance was ever officially adopted as law, it was unofficially applied to black occupancy in the town, defining where African Americans could rent and where they could buy land for decades to come.

By the 1930s, the black population had grown from five families and sixty-two people in 1920 to over 1,100, expanding to the south and east—the only directions allowed—to establish Carver Heights and what was called "Queen City" east of Avenue A and south of Nineteenth Street. The original neighborhoods were built and grew catch-as-catch-can. Not until the 1960s could African Americans in Lubbock obtain a mortgage to buy or a bank loan to repair a house. In her book *Remember When*, Katie Parks describes the pattern of growth in East Lubbock during the 1920s and early 1930s, when African Americans were first drawn to Lubbock primarily for the farm labor jobs available.

> They began to build make-shift homes with scrap lumber, tin, cardboard, and whatever else they could find to provide shelter. In the beginning, there were no sewer lines, and the early settlers used outside toilets, kerosene lamps, and wood and coal burning stoves. It was not until the late thirties that sewer lines, gas, and electricity were placed in East Lubbock. Electricity had been turned on in West Lubbock in 1916.[7]

Parks goes on to describe a series of petitions submitted to the city council in the 1940s for more fire hydrants, street lights, additional bus service, and water lines. A request for black policemen is also a continuing refrain. In 1992, when Parks completed the research on her book, she could list only four black police officers currently working for the city of Lubbock and a total of twenty-three in the whole history of the city from 1909 to 1992, with no black police officers hired in the 1940s or the 1970s. Until the 1960s, a black police officer in Lubbock was not allowed to arrest a white person, regardless of the offense.[8]

Bobbie Gean Bailey grew up at Eighteenth Street and Avenue B, in the heart of the Flats, guiding her grandmother about town while her mother worked. "Well, my grandmother lost her sight," Bobbie explains. "She had seen me, but she had never seen my sister right next to me. So as a result, I was my grandmother's eyes. I carried her wherever she wanted to go, and she didn't have anything to stop her. She went to church. We went anywhere. We didn't have a car, so we walked everywhere we went." Patterson adds that Bobbie's grandmother could cook, sew, and do virtually everything a sighted person was capable of doing.

Bobbie remembers growing up on the Eastside. "Most of the time, we would walk where we had to go or one or two people had a car. We had enough businesses. We didn't have any clothing businesses, but we had restaurants, barber shops, a drug store, dry cleaners, . . . you know, stuff like that. So, we were kept pretty much in our neighborhood. We were taken care of in our neighborhood."

Buying clothes was an exception to this segregated pattern of commercial exchange. Black people were allowed in some downtown clothing stores but with stipulations. Bobbie explains, "Here in Lubbock . . . at Hanna Pope [a downtown clothing store], we would go in the store and buy, but you couldn't try them on. See, that was the difference, you know, we couldn't try on the clothes." Black shoppers had to devise their own ways of evaluating whether the clothes would fit, and Bobbie explains that they solved the problem by using strings to measure every possible length to establish the proper size. Patterson supports her point by pantomiming invisible strings pulled out of his left fist with his right hand, saying, "Man, they had every length of string you could imagine!"

Bobbie adds another point to her memories of downtown Lubbock. "They had water fountains for coloreds and water fountains for whites, and they had a restroom for coloreds and a restroom for whites." She speaks with a tone of relief at the list of amenities she could find on the Eastside. "Oh, let me tell you about the movies. Let me tell you about where I was growing up. In my community, there were two movies, restaurants, and a beauty school. There were plenty of businesses, so we didn't suffer our whole lives for a lot of things."[9]

In an article titled "Black Lubbock," Robert L. Foster and Alwyn Barr describe the development of social organizations in East Lubbock. Besides an early interest in Christmas parties and the yearly Juneteenth celebration, "a Masonic Lodge was established in 1920, followed by the Knights of Pythias, and the Eastern Star about 1924. . . . In 1938 the Dunbar Parent-Teachers Association and another group of black citizens created two Boy Scout Troops. . . . During World War II, the American Legion organized Booker T. Washington Post 808 for black veterans in Lubbock.[10]

In many ways cultural life on the Eastside reflected the conventional norms of the rest of Lubbock, with the singular exception of the place of bootlegging in the dynamics of the black community. From 1901 on, Lubbock was a dry county and remained a place with no commercial access to liquor of any kind until 1960 when Lubbock County Precinct 2—home to the predominantly German-Catholic railroad town of Slaton—voted to sell alcohol. Liquor stores quickly popped up on the far edge of Precinct 2 as close as they could get to Lubbock, making the legal sale of packaged spirits readily available to the populace of that larger and ever-growing dry town. Before 1960 and the creation of "the Strip," as that neon-illuminated line of liquor stores soon became known, Lubbock had relied on a thriving bootleg industry that took many entrepreneurial forms.[11]

In 1940, when the population of Lubbock was not quite 32,000, the city newspaper ran an article reporting that "168,745 doctors' prescriptions for liquor had been issued in Lubbock during the period from December 1, 1939, to April 30, 1940."[12] Obviously, some physicians and some pharmacies had found a legal way to dispense alcohol "for medicinal purposes" to quite a few interested citizens, but it was through a vast bootlegging network that forbidden spirits became a lucrative occupation.

Patterson's aunt, April Rose, made a very successful career of bootlegging on the Eastside and was the first to explain to her nephew how things were in Lubbock. Patterson says, "She was tough back in the day when the Hispanic folk owned the east end of Broadway and the black folk [were] down there on Avenue A." Local bootleggers were supplied by out-of-town brokers from wet cities located primarily in Texas, Oklahoma, and New Mexico. They knew all the back roads of dry West Texas and delivered their goods in the dead of night. Local dealers on the Eastside often distributed their supply by wearing jackets lined with pockets, called "lugs," that could hold and transport ten half-pint bottles of alcohol. Some bootleggers wore two lug jackets on their bodies but had to exercise great caution to avoid breakage and the attention of the authorities. When Patterson arrived in town in 1958, half-pint bottles sold for three dollars each. Scores of college students purchased alcohol through drive-by kitchen windows in Queen City, using designated grocery passwords for the type of liquor they planned to purchase.

Patterson says the churches served as secure warehouses for packaged liquor. "When the benediction was said . . . and the sun was going down, alcohol came into their storerooms. The authorities would not raid the churches." He explains that the black bootleggers filled a desperate financial void, funding business enterprises, places of worship, and family needs in the black neighborhoods. Bootleggers offered a ready source of cash to a community that had no access to any kind of formal banking system. East Lubbock relied on the bootleggers, and the police often turned a blind eye to the illegality of these small, clandestine businesses, provided they remained small.[13] Out-of-town suppliers were another story altogether, and the night was filled with many a high-speed chase between local lawmen and downstate distributors coming and going through "the wettest dry town in the nation," as Lubbock was often described.[14]

Wichita Falls was then a little bit bigger than Lubbock and a little bit older, but it shared a similar settlement history and cultural sensibilities. Patterson was raised in the segregated black community of Wichita Falls after his mother moved there with him in 1939. She was originally from Waxahachie, Texas, a cotton town of around 8,000 people, located just south of Dallas. Patterson was born at four in the afternoon on Thursday, June 29, 1937, delivered by a midwife at a home across the street from the Joshua AME Church. African Americans were not allowed in Waxahachie hospitals in 1937. T. J. was named after his uncle Thomas James Collins and was the only child of Samuel Collins and his wife, Hannah Lee Barton Collins. Patterson's mother had just graduated from high school, which in those days only went to eleventh grade in black schools. The new mother was the eighteenth child of Harriet Mae White Barton and Henry Barton.

Patterson's mother and father separated and divorced soon after he was born, and his mother never talked to him about Samuel Collins. Mother and son were living in Waxahachie when the four-year-old boy was diagnosed with polio, a ravaging virus plaguing the whole world at this time. By attacking the nerve cells controlling muscle movement, the disease often caused death or crippled limbs to its victims. Even though President Franklin Roosevelt contracted polio as an adult, it was children who were especially vulnerable to the disease, and one of Patterson's aunts, Cora Lee Monroe, rushed from Detroit to aid his mother, taking them by train from Waxahachie to Wichita Falls, where better treatment was available.

Patterson was wrapped in a sheet for the trip. He could not sit up in bed, and his grandmother had secured his back to stiff cardboard, fabricating a hand-made brace to keep him upright and able to breathe during the train trip. In Wichita Falls, Patterson was one of six children under treatment, five white and one black. Of the six, five died. Only Patterson survived, and because he was African American, he notes, "the doctor had to come and see me where I was in a home down on Aiken Street."[15]

As with virtually everything else in the nation, medical treatment was rigidly segregated and woefully inadequate in African American communities. Even Franklin Roosevelt's Warm Springs, Georgia, polio rehabilitation center was for whites only. Medical discrimination, at least for polio, began to lift in 1941, when the Tuskegee Institute opened its Infantile Paralysis Center, with March of Dimes funding, to treat black polio victims and train black physicians and other health professionals in diagnostic and rehabilitation protocols for the disease. Until then, the broader community had just assumed that polio was a disease that struck white people, oblivious to the limited access that blacks had to doctors and hospitals and how inadequately trained black health care professionals were in diagnosing poliovirus in their patients. The Tuskegee Institute Infantile Paralysis

Center was for black victims. The Roosevelt Warm Springs Institute for Rehabilitation was for white victims. By the late 1940s the March of Dimes was using its funding to integrate training programs and health facilities, featuring black and white children on March of Dime posters and actively working to break down medical segregation.[16]

During Patterson's home-visit polio treatment, his grandmother stayed with his mother in Wichita Falls and put her energies into prayer. "Grandma was a praying woman," Patterson says. "She didn't believe in medicine." When his grandmother died in 1947, he says, "all those drugs that they prescribed for her were always on the cabinet. She didn't ever take none of it. She didn't believe in medicine. She believed in prayer." Patterson is very proud of the favor his grandmother showed him. She purchased an insurance policy for a dime a month to help him go to college. The cash value of the policy was $250. Patterson has never doubted that the force of her prayers had something to do with his recovery without disfigurement from the disease.[17]

It would take until 1955 for a vaccine to be developed and distributed, blocking the assault of poliovirus on the children of the world. Until then, the child killer and crippler continued its evil onslaught without regard to skin color or station in life. Each year, the school children of the nation participated in the annual March of Dimes fundraiser. Teachers would pass out cardboard forms with dime-sized circular depressions to be taken home and filled with dimes by the parents. Students were encouraged to participate in the fund drive through classroom posters of the year's March of Dimes poster child smiling in leg braces, leaning on crutches, or lying in an iron lung. Patterson managed to survive without enduring this device, and even if he had needed it, his race would certainly have kept him from access to the machine. White polio victims who needed help breathing were placed into the cylindrical steel drum of this horizontal construct. A door, allowing the child's head and neck to remain free, was then closed, forming a sealed, airtight compartment around the rest of the body. Pumps that controlled airflow decreased and increased the air pressure within the chamber to simulate normal breathing. This was essentially noninvasive therapy, but it was still a foreboding contraption, reminiscent of the laboratory machinery created by Hollywood mad scientists.

Parents lived in constant fear. As a home method of early polio diagnosis, they tested their children to see whether they could touch their chin to their chest and turn their head from side to side. Some parents refused to allow their children to have their tonsils removed, believing that the tonsils helped prevent polio. Summers were the most dangerous time for contracting the virus, and often physicians advised that children rest inside during the midday heat and only be allowed to go swimming after 3:00 p.m. as a defense against the disease. These were wild and desperate measures, feeble attempts to stave off the malady, but parents and medical professionals needed to feel they could do something to protect the children.[18]

Those who did contract polio were often segregated from the other children in the home and certainly the general public, for fear they were contagious. The disease certainly proceeded like a contagion. Lubbock newscaster Skip Watson was struck with polio in 1948 at age three, while living with his family at Lubbock's Reese Air Force Base. He remembers, "Everyone was getting it around me, twenty-four at Reese. Parents took me to the doctor, who said I had a bad case of the flu. As my muscles stiffened, they finally decided to look in a medical book or something and agreed it was polio." The Lubbock medical protocol was rather bewildering. "They sent everybody suffering from polio to Plainview to get them out of the population, since they had no idea what caused it," Watson explains with a shrug. "Guess they didn't care if Plainview folks got the problem."

Following his initial treatment in Plainview, Watson was transferred to Abilene, Texas, where they had adopted the treatment developed by the Australian nurse Sister Kenny, introduced in the United States in 1940. He explains: "That is where they put military blankets in scalding water and then wrapped you in them to decrease the pain and attempt to release muscles which had become stiff or constricted." From Abilene he was transferred to Scottish Rite Hospital in Dallas on the recommendation of Lubbock congressman George Mahon. It was there that Watson learned how to control the pain. "I developed a major trust in God," he says. "Scottish Rite provided no pain medication following surgery. They were fearful of addiction. When you came out of surgery you tolerated the pain. You mostly screamed!" He continues, "I was in and out of there for treatment until age thirteen—had seven operations. First time out of SR [Scottish Rite], I left with braces attached to high top shoes on both legs, brace on back, right hand and left arm with Canadian crutches." Watson's steady stream of twice-annual operations continued each year at Christmas and the beginning of the summer until his final operation at age sixteen, when he said, "No more. I was tired of all the cutting."[19]

While it came too late for Patterson and Watson, Dr. Jonas Salk discovered a cure for this insidious disease through his work in microbiology at New York University School of Medicine in conjunction with the President Franklin Delano Roosevelt National Institute for Infantile Paralysis. Through human tests that included the doctor and his family, Salk found that dead poliovirus cells successfully protected those inoculated from the crippling disease. When his success was made public in 1955, the good doctor became famous overnight for developing the Salk vaccine. He was hailed as a miracle worker and won the deep gratitude of parents all over the world when he refused to patent the vaccine to make sure it was distributed as quickly as possible. The results were lightning fast as children lined up in schools for this inexpensive inoculation. Today, thanks to the Salk vaccine and an energetic global inoculation initiative, polio has been virtually eradicated, with only twenty-nine cases reported worldwide in 2015 and as few as seventeen in 2016.[20]

After Patterson's miraculous recovery from infantile paralysis, his grandmother Barton returned to Waxahachie. His mother and he remained in Wichita Falls, and in 1940 Hannah Lee Barton Collins married Hershiel James Patterson, who legally adopted her three-year-old son and gave him his last name. From that day on, Thomas James Collins has proudly been Thomas James Patterson, gaining two half-sisters and a half-brother on the Patterson side: Doris Jean, Delorse, and Hershiel James, Jr. T. J. would be thirty-two years old before he met his biological father and stepmother, Dorothy Collins, who is seven years Patterson's senior and a retired principal from Edgewood Independent School District in San Antonio, Texas.

Hershiel Patterson is the only father that T. J. Patterson has ever known, and Patterson remembers his stepfather with gratitude and respect as a loving father and hard-working man, who was a bellhop when he married his mother. "One thing about him," Patterson says. "He would always work, always work. I think about him bringing us into the family like that. He didn't have to do that, but he did, and I appreciate that." Patterson's mother shared a similar drive and worked as a maid before becoming a beautician.[21]

Growing up in segregated Wichita Falls was very similar for Patterson as growing up in segregated Lubbock was for Bobbie. In a reminiscence of Wichita Falls in the 1950s, Randy Lewis observes that "black people . . . were virtually invisible in my childhood, living in a section of town east of the railroad tracks, going to their own schools, and trading with their own businesses. When they ventured into the downtown Kresge five-and-dime, they had their own restroom and used drinking fountains clearly labeled as 'colored.'"[22] For African Americans living in Wichita Falls, just as in Lubbock, the black neighborhood was the center of life.

When Patterson was around four years old, he met and became close friends with Elijah Donaldson, or E. J. Donaldson to his family and friends. Donaldson celebrates being raised in a tightly knit neighborhood where every adult you knew felt emboldened to administer corporal punishment. He says of Patterson, "All his life, he was raised in a community where everybody spanked your behind, if you got into trouble. . . . I think we'd get about five or six whippings coming from school before we even get home, and after we get home, there's two more."

Hershiel Patterson did his share of paddling the schoolboys, but Patterson's mother was the one who kept the books and tallied the score when delayed discipline was required. Donaldson explains, "She wasn't strict, but she ruled the house. . . . And, if she couldn't do it, she'd say, 'Hershiel, you got to see about that boy.' She would wait and . . . count up the whuppings. They'd say, 'I'm going to get you for such and such thing,' and let it go. Saturday: two, three, four, five, six whippings at one time. We'd tease each other about that. Oh man, T. J. would get mad."

After the punishment was given, the buddies would debate who got the most, but there is no debate between the two friends today about that old chestnut, "Spare the rod and spoil the child." Donaldson feels good about their upbringing. "Yeah," he says, "our school days was real good."

While Saturday whippings helped to "rear" the boys, Donaldson believes regular Sundays at church were also responsible for them turning out properly. "We went to Saint Matthew Baptist Church—were all baptized together," he says. "It was me, T. J., Homer Lindsey, and Tommy Williams. We all joined church at the same time. We were in the same age range between ten, eleven, or twelve. We couldn't stray too far away from each other, you know. I don't know why. We just kept in touch with one another."

In 1949 the family moved to New Jersey where Patterson's stepfather thought there would be better opportunities for a good job. It was an easy move for a gregarious fourth grader who sported an African top notch. "We grew our hair back," Patterson explains, "and we wore bangs." The better job turned out to be seasonal work as a soda jerk in Atlantic City from Memorial Day to Labor Day. After four years the family moved back to Wichita Falls and warmer weather.[23]

Patterson returned during his eighth-grade year, and time evaporated in young Donaldson's mind when Patterson's aunt announced the good news to her Wichita Falls neighbors. Donaldson remembers, "[T. J.'s] aunt lived on the corner from me. She said, 'Joanay, boy, T. J.'s coming home.'

'Boy,' I said, 'oh, man!'" When the family returned, the whole neighborhood turned out to greet them. "Well," he says, "when he come home . . . everybody in the neighborhood was elated. . . . It was just a thrill to see him. He was tall and skinny, and then, we just were having fun."

Donaldson insists that during his school years in Wichita Falls, Patterson was a leader, even when he struggled at times, as he did in choir and basketball. His school mate claims, "T. J. never could sing but he tried, same as basketball." Despite those two strikes against his extracurricular activities, Patterson was a standout in baseball. "That man could play some baseball," Donaldson continues. "But he was too slow; he'd have to hit a home run to make it down first base." Then he adds, "A good catcher, a very good catcher. He could throw that ball a hundred miles an hour."

Neither of these young men were fighters, but at a high-school Halloween dance, Patterson almost became one. Luckily, Donaldson was there with the humor necessary to hold him back. "It was Halloween," Donaldson begins. "He was going with this young lady, and he went as a cowboy. I think I was a cowboy too. We went to this party, and this other guy, a young man, was kissing his girlfriend.

"T. J. said, 'That joker kissed on my girlfriend. Hold my guns.'

"I said, 'What? T. J., you're a cowboy. Cowboys don't take their guns off to go to a fight. They keep them.'

"Oh, we laughed about that for years, but he never did fight. T. J. wasn't a fighter. None of us was a fighter. We always tried to talk our way out of it or, at least, I tried to."

When these two easy-going young men needed money, they earned it the old-fashioned way. They found a job. "We used to walk together going to work at the Casey drive-in," Donaldson says. "He used to wash dishes there. Miss Catherine Williams, a neighbor told him 'T. J., you keep doing what you're doing. Stay out of trouble, and you'll be proud of yourself.' We worked together at Faith Cafe. Then, we started working out at the Wichita Falls Country Club. Yeah, we was caddies. We'd walk to work and ride back home. . . . We'd always have fun."[24]

Patterson shares one story about his caddy experience that definitely was not fun. "You know," he says, "I was a caddy at the Wichita Falls Country Club and was standing near my player's bag when he said, 'Nigger, bring my bag.' Then, he looked at me and added, 'Let me scratch your head for good luck.' I was about fifteen, and all I could do was look at him. I was angry, but I had walked to the golf course to make a dollar fifty for caddying eighteen holes. If you made you three dollars, then you bought yourself two hamburgers for a quarter and rode the bus back for fifteen cents."

Patterson recalls when he and Donaldson were dishwashers, or "pearl divers" as they were called. Mattie Beavers taught him the trade. The caustic detergents in those pre-OSHA days cleaned the hair off his hands and arms, and Patterson's pay was $12.50 a week. The restaurant was owned by Sam Casdonia, a Greek who allowed black customers to enter and eat in the back of the establishment. One of Patterson's tasks was to see that the rear area was clean for the black patrons.[25]

Bobbie remembers these kinds of accommodations on school bus trips. "When we were in school traveling with the basketball team, we would go visit other schools, and they'd charter a bus for us. When we'd eat somewhere, or stop at a cafe, we'd have to eat in the back of the restaurant and go to the kitchen to get all of our food. We couldn't go into the front. . . . Same thing about the bus station downtown." She adds, "When you got on the bus, no matter how many people are on there, you had to go straight to the back, as far as you can get to the back. This is the whole time I was growing up."[26]

Donaldson likes to call T. J. Patterson the "Rosa Parks of Wichita Falls" because of a bus incident when they were in high school. "We were on the bus. That was before Martin Luther King, Jr., Rosa Parks—any of them—thought about integration and segregation. We were on the bus, and this lady told T. J. to get up. She wanted that seat. We all told T. J., 'Don't you move. Don't you let her sit there.' And she said, 'Did you hear me?' T. J. said, 'There's some seats up front. I want this seat!' We all stood up. There was about six of us. We just stood and said, 'You'd better go up front.'

"The bus driver came back and said, 'She can't sit back here.' He went up and told her to sit up front. So when the bus got close to . . . where we could get off and walk home, Tommy pulled the cord. He got off the bus, so we got off the bus with him. . . . He says, 'Man, if we go downtown, don't you know we'll go to jail?'"

Donaldson explains, "Yes, [if] that bus driver let us off the bus right there in the heart of Wichita Falls in downtown, all he had to do was holler at the policemen that was standing at the corner, and they would have jacked us up and carried us to jail."[27]

Interactions with the general white populace were always precarious affairs, fraught with insulting or violent possibilities. African Americans could attend the movies but were relegated to the balcony, totally separated from the white patrons, unless it was a late-night show. In *Remember When*, Katie Parks includes a reminiscence of segregated Lubbock with

Almo Sedberry, who was the owner of Sedberry's Barbershop, opened in 1937 and still operating in 1992. "During those times," he says, "there were midnight showings at the movie theater. Negroes had to sit in the balcony during the day, but at the midnight showing, you'd go up around 11:30 p.m. and sit anywhere." He explains that most of the people would stay after the show, and "that's when the trouble would start. At night, the police would just be waiting to arrest those walking home from the show because it would be after midnight." He goes on to explain that he owned a car and would often make two or three trips to the theater on Saturday nights to pick people up and keep them from being arrested for breaking the curfew placed on African Americans.[28]

Donaldson adds an ominous story his family spoke of in hushed tones. "My parents used to tell us about when they was coming up, things that was done to one of the family members—someone that they knew. I would say, 'What was it? What was it?' They say, 'You know anything about hanging?' I said, 'No.' She said, 'Well, we have seen this, and we're used to it, so that's why we stayed on the farm.'"[29]

With all these institutionalized efforts to keep African Americans in a fearful and subservient role in the culture, with all the laws and customs and attitudes, it is rather interesting to note that Patterson and his wife both had white relatives in their immediate families who were a meaningful part of their lives.

Bobbie knew very little about her biological father. Her mother remarried, and she explains, "I've seen my real daddy twice and my stepdaddy raised us. He was the only daddy I knew. . . . His name was H. S. Hutchinson—Hillary Samuel Hutchinson—but mother used to call him Hillary, for short. So that's what we called him." Bobbie is very proud to note that her stepfather was a member of the Lubbock Black Hubbers, a very talented semiprofessional baseball team that played minor-league ball throughout the region off and on from the 1930s through the 1950s. Hillary Samuel Hutchinson's father was white, and Bobbie explains her understanding of white people in this racially divided world of her youth. "When we were coming up, we lived in the Flats. We were poor. We didn't even know. We thought everybody was poor. There was an Anglo boy I grew up with. We talked . . . and laughed. I went to his graduation, birthday parties. He came to my house, so I didn't have a negative attitude about white people. They were just like everybody else, as far as I was concerned. My stepdaddy's daddy, he was white so 'whatever.'"[30]

Patterson's grandfather, Henry Barton, was a white man too. Harriet

Mae White, whom Patterson calls his "little short grandmother," was a former slave, born in 1862 in North Carolina. She grew up in the turmoil of North Carolina during Reconstruction, then moved to Waxahachie, Texas, and married Henry Barton, a white German house builder. Interracial marriage was illegal in Texas and fifteen other states until 1967, when the US Supreme Court ruled in *Loving v. Virginia* that miscegenation laws were unconstitutional. Nevertheless, Patterson insists, his grandparents were married, perhaps through a special church ceremony, some eighty years before that ruling. "Yes, sir," he says. "They were legally married, man and wife, black and white, collectively having eighteen boys and girls together." He goes on to observe: "Yeah, a lot of folks in Waxahachie had white granddaddies. You'd be surprised. It might a been against the law, but it was kind of clannish. . . . Outsiders didn't come in and tell folks, as I understand it, what they could and could not do."

Patterson is convinced that the influence of his white grandfather on the physician caring for him when he had polio made all the difference in the quality of his treatment. The doctor attended to him with great concern through consistent home visits, a rare kind of medical attention for black people in 1939 Texas. He characterizes his grandfather Barton as a strong, well-liked man and a talented athlete. "He was a boxer . . . , and he played ball for the Saint Louis Cardinals farm club . . . in Waxahachie." A "southpaw," he adds. However, no amount of athleticism or likeability could overcome the rigid racial divisions of the culture, starting with Henry Barton's family. Patterson says, "The family members were very unhappy with Grandpa because he had married this black woman. . . ." He then repeats a timeworn tale: "My cousin always told the story. She was about twenty years older than me. She said the guards would come by night and Grandma and Grandpa had to go out into the cotton field, and they'd lay down. See, they'd shoot at them. . . . His sisters and brothers didn't like what he had done. They wanted to kill him."

Patterson also shares the family's favorite story about the racial divide, starring nineteen-year-old Aunt April Rose. This much-heralded episode happened in 1938, when Grandfather Barton was visiting his daughter April Rose in Lubbock. "She was a talker," Patterson says. "I believe it was in the Flats. . . . When someone came by with white pigmentation, they stood out and, of course, it was against the rules in those days." As father and daughter took a stroll down Avenue G, this very unusual sight caught the attention of the police, and they quickly tried to arrest April Rose. Whatever they suspected might be happening between a young black woman and an older white man, April Rose immediately set them straight. She defiantly proclaimed, "But, this is my daddy," and accompanied her loud protest with a steady stream of invective. The nonplussed policemen backed off and moved on, rather than debate either the father or his fiery-tongued daughter.

The family loved to retell this story of a very young black woman standing up to the law, and it certainly wasn't the only time. April Rose was well known as a person who could handle almost any challenge that life threw her. Once she was brought up before a judge for bootlegging, and she kept cussing at the judge until her contempt charges had reached one thousand dollars. Then she became silent and just paid the fine. "She was daring," Patterson says with admiration and affection. "You didn't frighten her, but they wanted to arrest her for walking with her daddy!"[31]

Actually, in 1938 a young black woman could have very well been arrested for walking down Avenue G with an older white man. For African Americans in Jim Crow Texas, law enforcement was a white institution, imposed capriciously on black people any time they ventured beyond the narrow confines of their defined territory or just caught the attention of a policeman for some unknown reason. It was only in the home and the neighborhood that black people could consistently find a safe haven, in circumstances where family and friends took their jobs as watchdogs and disciplinarians seriously.

Bobbie and T. J. Patterson were a part of the last generation of African Americans to experience the strictures of institutionalized racial segregation. While the similarities in their upbringing gave them a foundation of shared values and experience, they were straddling two worlds when they married in 1960. The segregated culture they had known growing up in Lubbock and Wichita Falls was rapidly changing. Through the growing momentum of the civil-rights movement, interpretations of federal law in support of black citizens were being established at every turn, and the Pattersons began their marriage with the confidence that they would build a promising future for themselves that their grandparents and parents could never have possibly imagined.

The newlyweds settled into a happy and comfortable new life together in their first home, a duplex in the 600 block of East Twenty-third Street. Bobbie took a position as a substitute teacher at Ralls Independent School District, and Patterson returned to his responsibilities at the Mary and Mac School. Soon, Avis Elise and Thomas James, Jr., were born very close together, and life moved along in an exhausting but contented way as they juggled the demands of their jobs and the needs of their babies. Then, out of the blue, T. J. was drafted into the US Army, and Bobbie faced the dire prospects of caring for the children all alone on a decidedly diminished income.[32]

T. J.'s grandparents, Harriett Barton and Henry Barton, early 1950s.

Henry Barton family, eleven of T. J. Patterson's eighteen aunts and uncles, Waxahachie, Texas, 1950s. Back row: Cecil Graves, Lucille Barton Graves, April Rose Barton, Thad Barton, Cora Lee Barton, Hannah Barton (T. J.'s mother), and Elder Willie Barton. Front row: G. B. Barton, Theresa Barton, Annie Mae Barton, Herman Barton.

Henry Barton, home builder, early 1960s.

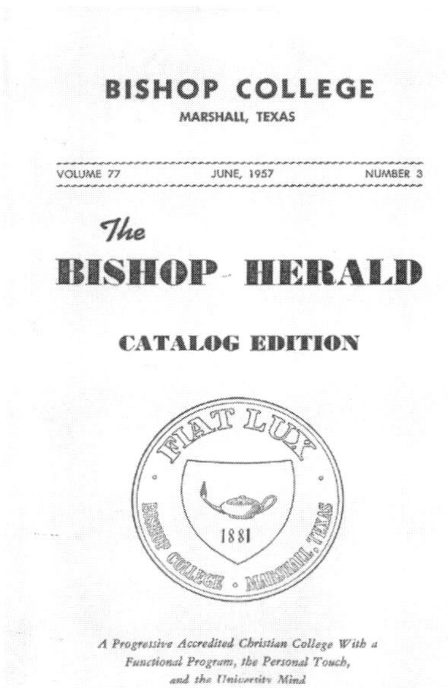

BISHOP COLLEGE
MARSHALL, TEXAS

VOLUME 77 JUNE, 1957 NUMBER 3

The
BISHOP HERALD

CATALOG EDITION

FIAT LUX
1881
BISHOP COLLEGE · MARSHALL, TEXAS

A Progressive Accredited Christian College With a Functional Program, the Personal Touch, and the University Mind

T. J. Patterson graduates from Bishop College, May 23, 1958 (courtesy of Paul Quinn College, Dallas, Texas).

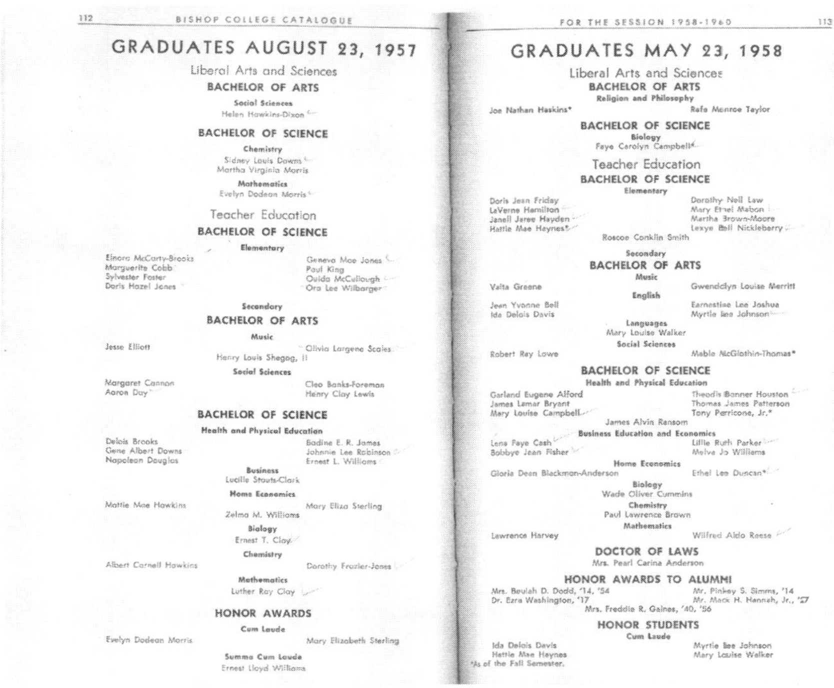

112 BISHOP COLLEGE CATALOGUE

GRADUATES AUGUST 23, 1957

Liberal Arts and Sciences

BACHELOR OF ARTS

Social Sciences

Helen Hawkins-Dixon

BACHELOR OF SCIENCE

Chemistry

Sidney Louis Downs
Martha Virginia Morris

Mathematics

Evelyn Dodean Morris

Teacher Education

BACHELOR OF SCIENCE

Elementary

Einora McCarty-Brooks
Marguerite Cobb
Sylvester Foster
Doris Hazel Jones
Geneva Mae Jones
Paul King
Ouida McCullough
Ora Lee Wilbarger

Secondary

BACHELOR OF ARTS

Music

Jesse Elliott
Olivia Largene Scales
Henry Louis Shegog, II

Social Sciences

Margaret Cannon
Aaron Day
Cleo Banks-Foreman
Henry Clay Lewis

BACHELOR OF SCIENCE

Health and Physical Education

Delois Brooks
Gene Albert Downs
Napolean Douglas
Badine E. R. James
Johnnie Lee Robinson
Ernest L. Williams

Business

Lucille Stouts-Clark

Home Economics

Mattie Mae Hawkins
Mary Eliza Sterling
Zelma M. Williams

Biology

Ernest T. Clay

Chemistry

Albert Cornell Hawkins
Dorothy Frazier-Jones

Mathematics

Luther Ray Clay

HONOR AWARDS

Cum Laude

Evelyn Dodean Morris
Mary Elizabeth Sterling

Summa Cum Laude

Ernest Lloyd Williams

FOR THE SESSION 1958-1960 113

GRADUATES MAY 23, 1958

Liberal Arts and Sciences

BACHELOR OF ARTS

Religion and Philosophy

Joe Nathan Haskins*
Rafe Monroe Taylor

BACHELOR OF SCIENCE

Biology

Faye Carolyn Campbell*

Teacher Education

BACHELOR OF SCIENCE

Elementary

Doris Jean Friday
LaVerne Hamilton
Janell Jaree Hayden
Hattie Mae Haynes*
Dorothy Nell Law
Mary Ethel Mabon
Martha Brown-Moore
Lexye Bell Nickleberry
Roscoe Conklin Smith

Secondary

BACHELOR OF ARTS

Music

Valta Greene
Gwendolyn Louise Merritt

English

Jean Yvonne Bell
Ida Delois Davis
Earnestine Lee Joshua
Myrtle lee Johnson

Languages

Mary Louise Walker

Social Sciences

Robert Rey Lowe
Mable McGlothin-Thomas*

BACHELOR OF SCIENCE

Health and Physical Education

Garland Eugene Alford
James Lemar Bryant
Mary Louise Campbell
Theodis Bonner Houston
Thomas James Patterson
Tony Perricone, Jr.*
James Alvin Ransom

Business Education and Economics

Lena Faye Cash
Bobbye Jean Fisher
Lillie Ruth Parker
Melva Jo Williams

Home Economics

Gloria Dean Blackmon-Anderson
Ethel Lee Duncan*

Biology

Wade Oliver Cummins

Chemistry

Paul Lawrence Brown

Mathematics

Lawrence Harvey
Wilfred Aldo Reese

DOCTOR OF LAWS

Mrs. Pearl Carina Anderson

HONOR AWARDS TO ALUMNI

Mrs. Beulah D. Dodd, '14, '54
Dr. Ezra Washington, '17
Mr. Pinkey S. Simms, '14
Mr. Mack H. Hannah, Jr., '27
Mrs. Freddie R. Gaines, '40, '56

HONOR STUDENTS

Cum Laude

Ida Delois Davis
Hattie Mae Haynes
Myrtle lee Johnson
Mary Louise Walker

*As of the Fall Semester.

Following wedding reception at Bethel AME Church, August 19, 1960, Lubbock, Texas; throwing rice, an emptied gasoline tank and "fool" written on side of car.

Bobbie Gean and T. J. Patterson wedding reception, Curtis Gibson, Virgil Smith, Virgil Johnson, T. J. Patterson, Bobbie Gean Bailey, Sara Bailey, Peggy Bailey, Shirley Mooney, and Sandra Hutchinson.

"Good Mamma" Sarah Crawford, Bobbie Gean's grandmother, blinded in her early 40s, owner of the Mickey Mouse Club.

Bobbie Gean and T. J. Patterson's children. Standing: Avis; seated: T. J., Jr., and Shelia, mid-1960.

Basic training at Fort Hood, Texas, 2nd Armored Division, "Hell on Wheels," 1961.

Downtown Danang, Vietnam, 1962. Inscription on back reads, "To my Wife Bobbie, From your Husband T. J."

Danang, Vietnam, 1962. Inscription on back reads, "To Avis and Tommie, From Daddie. (Daddie loves both of you) (Say a prayer for me)."

Danang, Vietnam, 1962. Inscription on back reads, “Daddie at the beach (smile). The sun nearly burnt me to death, smile. I was trying to get a suntan.”

Danang, Vietnam, 1962. Inscription on back reads, “To: Avis, Tommie and Bobbie Patterson, From Daddy. Danang. Vietnam. CHO-COA.”

T. J. Patterson, assistant dean in College of Business, Texas Technological College, Lubbock, Texas, 1979–1984.

Bobbie Gean and T. J. Patterson, 1970s.

April Rose Barton Hobdy funeral, Ford Memorial Church of God in Christ, Lubbock Texas, 1983. Front row (kneeling): Erica Hutchinson, Hillary Hutchinson III, Daniel Patterson, Zairreus Patterson, Marcus Williams, Gabriel Patterson, Michael McKinzie, Timothy Graves. Second row (kneeling): Leroy Cleaver, Shelia Patterson Harris, Melvin McKenzie. Standing: E. J. Donaldson, Shirley Patterson, Sara Blocker, Will Block, Gloria Cleaver, Robert Anderson, Michael Johnson, Evelyn Johnson, Roversa Mitchell, Debra Chatman, T. J. Patterson, Jr., Julius Graves, Hillary Hutchinson, Jr., Delores Robinson, John Hunter, Doris Gean Patterson, Luckey Cleaver, Theresa Rotchie, T. J. Patterson, Sr., Lucille Graves, Norma Faye Anderson, Bobbie Patterson, Toni Patterson-Edwards.

Official portrait of Lubbock City Councilman T. J. Patterson, District Two, elected April 4, 1982, first African American to hold this position.

Congressman Emanuel Cleaver, 14th Congressional District, Kansas City, Missouri (T. J. Patterson's second cousin) congratulates T. J. on his election as Lubbock's first African American city councilman, April 4, 1984.

Bobbie Gean and T. J. Patterson, 1980s.

Councilman T. J. Patterson at Lubbock Lake Site #6, Spring 1990, Lubbock, Texas.

Sam Collins, T. J.'s biological father, Lubbock, Texas, 1992.

Dedication of Bobbie Gean and T. J. Patterson Library, Lubbock, Texas, December 1995.

Attending Texas Municipal League, 1998. Standing L to R: Zairreus D. Patterson, T. J. Patterson Jr., Ursula Patterson holding T. J. Patterson III, Shawn Harris, Shelia P. Harris, Asya Harris. Seated: Bobbie Gean Patterson, T. J. Patterson, Sr.

T. J. Patterson (in dashiki clothing), Mayor Windy Sitton, and mascot to the Lubbock Crickets semi-pro baseball team.

Mayor Alan Henry and T. J. Patterson at McInturff Conference Center, Lubbock, Texas, September 4, 2002.

T. J. Patterson, Mayor Marc McDougal, and Eddie Richardson at twenty-fifth anniversary celebration of *Southwest Digest* newspaper, September 4, 2002.

Eddie Richardson at twenty-fifth anniversary celebration of *Southwest Digest* newspaper, September 4, 2002.

Partners T. J. Patterson and Eddie Richardson at twenty-fifth anniversary celebration of *Southwest Digest* newspaper, September 4, 2002.

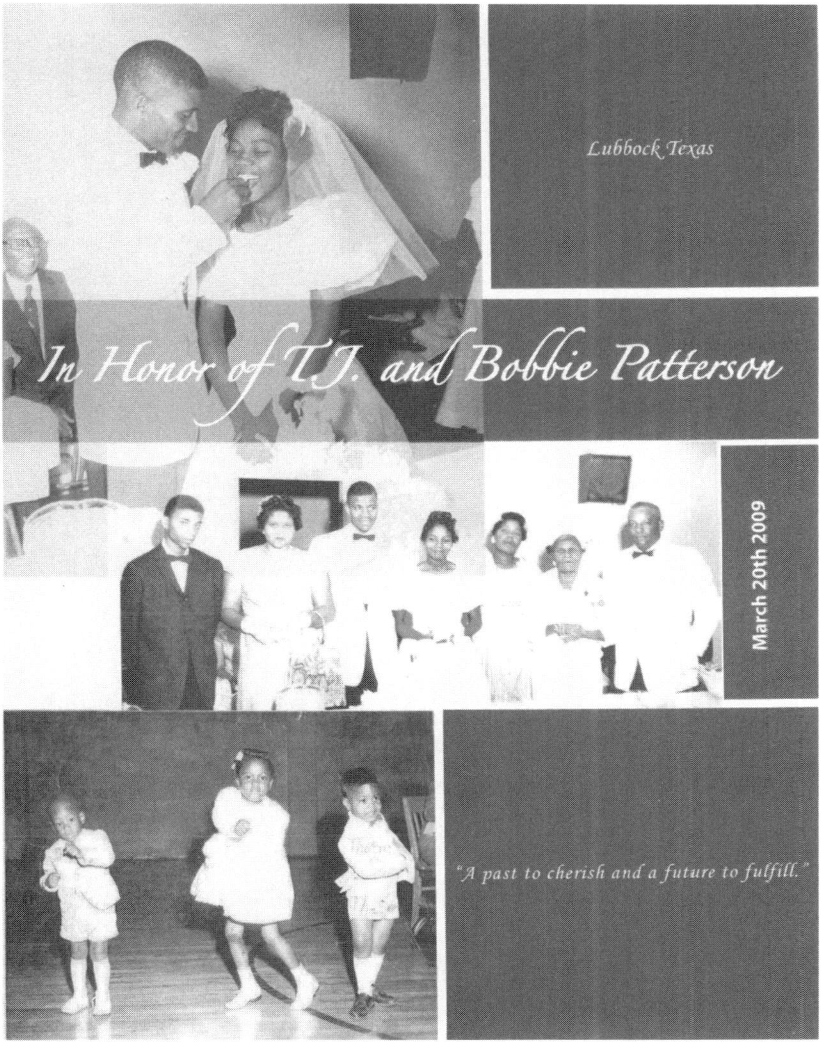

Front page of fiftieth anniversary program in honor of Bobbie Gean and T. J. Patterson's wedding, Holiday Inn, Lubbock, Texas, March 20, 2009.

Page from *Southwest Digest*, "In Honor of T. J. and Bobbie Patterson."

Chapter 3

"The Times They Are A-Changin'"

T. J. Patterson was drafted in September of 1961 and sent to army basic training at Fort Hood outside Killeen, Texas. Bobbie was left in Lubbock with the two babies. She explains the challenge. "I had to move back home with my grandmother. He had to move to the army post. That left us with only one check because I was working, driving back and forth to Ralls, Texas. I had two kids by that time. I was just barely able to pay for the car." Remembering those times, she emphasizes the importance of family. "It wasn't more than one hundred dollars a month," she says of Patterson's basic training pay. "But living with my grandmother helped me a lot. My mother was here, and my sister was here. I was a schoolteacher, so I was making [it]. As long as I could work, I was making pretty good. We were still living with my grandmother, so I didn't have a lot of rent to pay.[1]

After boot camp at Fort Hood, Patterson was sent to Fort Gordon in Augusta, Georgia, for Signal Corps training. This was his first extended experience outside the protective environments of home and school. He talks about this trip heading into unfamiliar territory. "I get on the bus in Lubbock with my white brother who is going to the same school. We're both sitting up front all the way to Dallas, where we changed buses but keep the same seats on the new bus. Then we get to Bossier City, Louisiana, outside of Shreveport, where a white woman gets on the bus. She walked up to where we're both sitting and said, 'I don't want this nigger sitting here.' My white brother turned his head, looked up and said, 'Ma'am, he's with me.' He looked her in the face, but I learned something. We're not far removed from the problem."[2]

It must have been the military uniform that saved these two soldiers from greater repercussions for sitting next to each other on a bus traveling through the South. At this very moment in time, the Freedom Rides were in full swing, blatantly challenging segregated travel, and there these two young men sat, right up front together on their way to Georgia.

President Harry S. Truman had integrated all military services in 1948, and the last all-black army unit was disbanded in 1954. By the 1960s army drill sergeants had adopted an introductory catch phrase they barked at all new recruits: "In the army, there is only one color—Green!" Black soldiers and white soldiers studied together, worked together, ate together, and traveled together,[3] but wherever they possibly could, the southern states were still enforcing strict segregation policies, and a black man sitting next to a white man on a national bus line was a deeply charged and highly dangerous situation. September of 1961 marked the fourth month of a coordinated, nonviolent protest that called on the Interstate Commerce Commission to enforce federal desegregation laws despite local Jim Crow rules in the South.

Led by James Farmer of CORE and soon joined by SNCC and SCLC, the Freedom Rides began on May 4, 1961, when seven black and six white passengers boarded a Greyhound bus in Washington, DC, traveling through Alabama and Mississippi to end the ride in New Orleans, Louisiana. Freedom Riders got on that bus in purposeful defiance of the customs of segregated bus travel, recently declared unconstitutional again in the 1960 *Boynton v. Virginia* decision, which reaffirmed the 1946 decision in *Morgan v. Commonwealth of Virginia*. On this first Freedom Ride, black people rode beside white people in the front of the bus. The riders included both men and women, ranging in age from eighteen to fifty. In their seating arrangements, they mixed genders and age with race. Black and white men and women also sat together in the bus terminal waiting rooms and ate together in bus terminal restaurants.

The reaction to the first Freedom Ride was far more violent than anyone had anticipated, and the melee shocked the nation. It all began on Mother's Day in Anniston, Alabama, where the local Ku Klux Klan, aided by the Anniston police commissioner, attacked two Greyhound buses carrying Freedom Riders. The Klansmen slit the bus tires and firebombed the vehicle, then held the doors shut as the bus burned. Only through an explosion—maybe a fuel tank, maybe a gunshot—did the riders escape. They were then beaten by the mob and only prevented from being lynched by the warning shots of Alabama highway patrolmen. Fearing reprisals, the hospitals refused to treat the wounded. Sympathetic black citizens helped them, and the Freedom Riders proceeded to Birmingham, where they were again greeted by the Klan, this time directly aided by the infamous segregationist, Birmingham Police Commissioner Bull Conner. The riders were beaten with baseball bats, iron pipes, and bicycle chains, with white males being singled out for the most vicious attacks. Again, the hospitals refused treatment.[4]

The national press covered this protest, and the violent reaction to the riders quickly generated international outrage, embarrassing the White House during a volatile time of rising Cold War tensions. John F. Kennedy had just become president of the United States on January 20, 1961, and this first Freedom Ride came less than a month after the Bay of Pigs invasion, where 1,400 CIA-trained Cuban exiles landed on the beaches of Cuba to instigate an uprising and overthrow the Castro regime. The invasion was a complete debacle from naval support to air cover to equipment and ammunition losses to troop confusion on the ground. After only three days of fighting, on April 20, 1961, the invaders surrendered to Fidel Castro's Revolutionary Armed Forces. Some of the invaders were executed, and the rest became prisoners of war. Ultimately, the United States negotiated an exchange of 1,113 of these Miami-based Cuban refugees for $53 million in food and medicine. This CIA-driven military failure was so strategically unsound that it became the salient example for the psychological study of the "groupthink syndrome," and Kennedy never again trusted final decision making to the Pentagon.[5]

While he had made a strong commitment to racial equality, Kennedy did not welcome a display of shocking domestic conflict on the heels of the humiliating Bay of Pigs invasion, and Attorney General Robert Kennedy appealed to the Freedom Riders for restraint. However, civil-rights leaders knew the momentum was with the riders and determined to continue. In spite of the hostility and violence, CORE and SNCC were able to recruit more and more "outside agitators" to travel to Alabama and Mississippi throughout the summer, and the Kennedy administration took on the responsibility of pressuring the governors of Alabama and Mississippi to provide state police and state national-guard protection for the riders.

To pass his New Frontier agenda combating poverty and racial discrimination, Kennedy needed the support of southern Democrats, who were uniformly hostile to the civil-rights movement in all its forms. Trying to avoid sending federal troops into the South by walking a fine line between protecting individual rights and respecting states' rights, Attorney General Robert Kennedy struck a bargain. If these decidedly unsympathetic governors would protect the riders as they traveled the highways of the South, the local police could arrest them for breaking Jim Crow laws when they reached their destination. The Freedom Riders soon came to understand that they would be jailed automatically for their behavior, so they adopted what became known as the "jail-no-bail" strategy. They just stayed in jail, making their incarceration part of the protest statement. From June through September of 1961, more than sixty Freedom Rides crisscrossed the South, with the riders defying a cadre of Jim Crow rules.[6]

Patterson was traveling with his white army companion on a Greyhound bus headed through the South in the thick of these Freedom Rides, and that hostile white woman on the bus taught him to beware. "All the way from Bossier City, Louisiana, to Fort Gordon, Georgia, I didn't get off that bus," he says. "I had a uniform on. What I am saying was we were not far removed from the problems. But you still love the United States of America."

During his Advanced Individual Training (AIT) with the Signal Corps, Patterson was able to go back to Lubbock and return with his wife and baby son, Tommy. Once again, the long road trip through the South was an unnerving experience. "When we left home, driving back to Georgia," Patterson says, "I wouldn't go in the store. She'd go buy something. Black folk had a hard time driving a red convertible going to Georgia."[7]

Bobbie was wary too. "We avoided restrooms a lot of places," she says. "When we were going through Mississippi, they were really nice. They gave you water to warm the baby's bottles, all that kind of stuff. . . . We had to stop. We stopped at a motel in Alabama. One time we just stopped on the side of the road because there were no motels for blacks anywhere. . . . I guess we were really in danger most of the time. I didn't know it. We stopped. They'd sell us gas, but we couldn't go to the restroom. They'd say they didn't have one."[8]

Patterson's friend, Elijah Donaldson, joined the army about the same time Patterson served and remembers an incident in North Carolina that points out the great difference between racial relations on base and off base during that time. To Donaldson Fort Bragg was especially difficult for a black serviceman. "The first time I went to town," he remembers, "I went with two guys in my barracks, Jerry and Allen. They were white.

"They said, 'Come go to the laundromat with us.' I said, 'Okay,' so we went downtown to the laundromat, and he parked in front, and I'm curious, and I thought I saw a sign that said, 'White Only.' So I said, 'Oh, I'll just sit in the car.' 'No, come on, let's go.' So we almost got in a confrontation with the manager because I was standing there. He comes out and says, 'What are you doing here?' I says, 'Who? I'm just with my friends.' He said, 'No, you got to leave.' So he just kept raising his voice and got louder and louder. 'I'm going to call the police!' So Jerry says, 'So call the police!' So . . . it was four women in there washing, and they just stopped washing, got their clothes and left. He told them, 'Oh no, you don't have to leave.' They said, 'No, we'll leave.' Of course, they were married to military personnel. So I went out and sit in the car, and he called the police. I was sitting there and saw this police car come up, and a guy got out and ran by, and I said, 'Oh Lord, I'm going to jail, and I'm going to die.' That was the biggest policeman I've ever seen in my life. But he was ex-military, and . . . says, 'Don't worry about nothing. . . . What's your rank?' I say, 'I'm a PFC.' He says, 'That's all right, Private First Class, just move your car across the street because this guy is just a dumb-butt. We have had conflict with him.' So I drove the car across the street until they finished their washing."

This kind of incident was not that unusual for black soldiers stationed in the South, and soon the US military officially addressed the issue. On July 26, 1963, Secretary of Defense Robert McNamara authorized Department of Defense Directive 5120.36, which expanded the military's responsibility to eliminating off-base discrimination, citing its detrimental consequences on the military effectiveness of black servicemen. That laundromat confrontation has always remained an unpleasant memory for Donaldson. "I just did not like Fayetteville, North Carolina," he says.[9]

In spite of the racial tensions as they traveled to Georgia, both Bobbie and T. J. were excited at the prospect of living in the hometown of famous blues performer James Brown. When they arrived, however, their first living quarters were very bad. "Let me tell you about Georgia," Bobbie exclaims. "We were in Augusta. We lived in an old hotel they had renovated, in an upstairs place. We had big sewage rats. We lived upstairs. They'd crawl up the walls, and we'd have to walk all over their [waste]." One night they had to chase away a rat boldly heading for their sleeping baby's crib.

Patterson says they were "intelligent rats." Bobbie says they were "hungry rats and that was the reason I got a fan." She explains, "In order to keep the rats from coming in, I bought a big old oscillating fan . . . an old thrashing fan and put it in front of the door. And when they'd go past it, it'd scare them off. They wouldn't come in at night. I had the baby, Tommy, so that's how we kept the rats away. . . . T. J. would leave us there during the day because he would drive the car."

Eventually they moved to safer quarters, and Bobbie was able to augment their income by substitute teaching. "For me, it was junior high school, high school, and elementary schools all on the same street," she says. "I started subbing there. The lady next door started babysitting, keeping my baby for me while I'd go substitute teach."

Patterson says, "She was part of the military too. I was her spouse."

The army was a completely new experience for him, but Bobbie's father had served in the Pacific during World War II, and she was familiar with life in the service. She remembers her dad serving in Okinawa, Japan, Myrtle Beach, South Carolina, and an army post in Arizona where the family once visited him. "He was in the army, so he left me, my mother, my sister, and grandmother at home while he went overseas. . . . My granddaddy and my grandmother had separated . . . so it was just the four of us there that I had growing up." She points out, "Well, it was totally segregated, completely segregated. The blacks were all just one. You know at that time, there was the fact that it was segregated, but I think of it as that they were happy being together, being in with their own group. So it wasn't nearly as bad as what people would think. It wasn't something they couldn't do. . . . USO for blacks and then for whites, basically saying that we were there; we weren't together."[10]

By the 1960s black and white soldiers were definitely together, stationed in West Germany—where the Soviets had built the Berlin Wall—and joined in the jungles of Southeast Asia. Bobbie returned to Lubbock at the end of Signal Corps Training, and Patterson was sent to Vietnam as part of the initial US buildup to an undeclared war against insurgent forces trying to topple the sitting South Vietnamese government. Patterson was in the country for thirteen months as a part of the Military Assistance Advisory Group (MAAG), the military arm assigned to train the South Vietnamese Army (ARVN forces).[11]

The United States had been supporting the South Vietnamese government since 1950, when Vietnam was still a French colony and one of the early hot spots of the great Cold War divide between Western democracies and Soviet-inspired communist regimes. In 1954 the French were roundly defeated at Dien Bien Phu by the communist Vietnamese and the subsequent Geneva Accords divided the country into communist North Vietnam and Western-aligned South Vietnam. The United States increased its support for South Vietnam and continued to supply weapons, advisors, finances, and ultimately troops to the government as the communist forces grew in strength over the years.[12]

Shortly after he landed there, Patterson witnessed the bombing of the

Presidential Palace in Saigon. "I got to Vietnam in February of 1962. I'm in the Majestic Hotel, waterfront out here; look across the water and see a Coca-Cola [sign]. I see these planes coming and bombing the palace. I'm looking and I say, 'What the heck is going on?' I was already shook up because when we landed, thousands of people came to see those 707s land at Tan Son Nhat Airport," he says. "When the planes land, they rush you off and put you in a bus to the Majestic Hotel. I saw the bombs coming down on the palace. I saw it."[13]

Later he learned the attack was by two South Vietnamese air force officers in a failed coup attempt on their own president, Ngo Dinh Diem, the autocratic leader of the Republic of Vietnam since 1955. To defend internal and external threats to his regime, Diem had implemented a series of aggressive policies directed at his opponents and any suspected communist. By 1958, some 40,000 political prisoners had been jailed or placed under house arrest, and over 12,000 had been killed. In 1960, in response to Diem's policing policies, the North Vietnam government in Hanoi authorized the use of an armed insurgency in the south, with South Vietnamese communists establishing the National Liberation Front or Viet Cong to overthrow the Diem regime. They built their organized resistance in the Mekong Delta and their supply line from North Vietnam on the Ho Chi Minh Trail winding through Laos and Cambodia to South Vietnam.

In response to this escalation of communist insurgency, the United States increased its support for South Vietnam. When Patterson arrived in 1962, there were 3,205 US troops in Vietnam. When he left in March of 1963, there were over 11,300 US troops already flying missions, accompanying ARVN units into battle and defoliating the jungle trails with Agent Orange. The seeds of doubt concerning this intervention were also already in place. On February 14, 1962, journalist James Reston wrote for the *New York Times*, "The United States is now involved in an undeclared war in South Vietnam. This is well known to the Russians, the Chinese communists, and everybody else concerned except the American people. . . . Has the President made clear to the Congress and the nation the extent of the U.S. commitment to the South Vietnam government and the dangers involved?" Senator Wayne Morse of Oregon echoed these same concerns in a closed Senate hearing on February 20. "When the ships start coming back to the west coast with the flat-draped coffins of American boys, look out, because the American people, in my judgment, are going to be very much divided." On February 26, a *Newsweek* article asked, "Will the sending of U.S. troops lead to escalation, more guerrillas, more Americans, and an eventual confrontation of the U.S. and Red China? Above all, can the U.S. strategy win the war?"[14]

The two air force pilots had hoped to kill Diem and his family and bring about an uprising of the South Vietnamese people against the authoritarian rule of the Diem regime. While they failed in 1962, Diem and his brother, Ngo Dinh Nhu, were assassinated in November of the next year, following a successful coup led by South Vietnamese generals. Perhaps for the US public, the first awareness of Vietnam as a crisis area came earlier in 1963, when Vietnamese Buddhists rose up in protest over flag flying during religious holidays. Diem had allowed Catholic flags but prohibited Buddhist flags, a symbolic indication of the Diem regime's treatment of the Buddhist majority in South Vietnam.

Unarmed civilians were killed during the flag flying protest, and the uprising escalated. As the ultimate expression of outrage, a Buddhist monk set himself on fire in the middle of a Saigon street, followed by other blazing suicides by Buddhist monks. Diem's sister-in-law, the powerful and haughty Madam Nhu, responded to the burnings by stating, "If the Buddhists want to have another barbecue, I will be glad to supply the gasoline." Footage of Buddhist monks in orange robes setting fire to themselves in the middle of an urban street was seen around the world. This was the dramatic and incomprehensible phenomenon that introduced the US public to South Vietnam, followed by the callous remarks of Madam Nhu, who served as the South Vietnamese First Lady.

At the time of the assassination of her brother-in-law and husband later that year, Madam Nhu was on a lecture tour in the United States, railing against the US government and the Buddhist monks, who she claimed were communists. She was a fearless and arrogant personality, often called the "Dragon Lady," who was forced into exile in France with the fall of the family regime. After the assassination of Diem and his brother, which the United States did not precipitate or prevent, South Vietnam never again had a stable, independent government.[15]

In February of 1962, the US presence in Vietnam was still a covert mission, and Patterson wore civilian clothes because the US Army was officially there only in an advisory role. He was a cryptographer and worked in a communication center, sending and decrypting messages as his Military Occupation Specialty (MOS): "We could send a message through a mountain peak rather than sending it to a satellite and then bouncing it to a target," Patterson explains. "A message from the jungle in Da Nang, South Vietnam, to Hawaii and then to the Pentagon in Washington, DC."

While he was not a combat solider and his unit was only responsible for protecting communications, the war spun around him. Patterson remembers his early days in-country. "I didn't know what a Viet Cong was until one day I was in downtown Da Nang, and they said everybody had to stop because Viet Cong was in the area. That was quite an experience, man. You didn't know if you were going to get back to America or not."[16]

The Viet Cong were masters at guerrilla warfare. They dressed and behaved like villagers and recruited one-on-one in the countryside. They built elaborate tunnels and camouflage structures in the jungles. They knew how to hide and challenge the effectiveness of conventional warfare. Kennedy recognized the importance of developing counterinsurgency tactics and in 1962 designated the Green Berets for that purpose. The US military, however, was too wedded to its tried-and-true ways to significantly change its approach to warfare. The United States plunged deeper and deeper into the conflict, dedicated to winning the war with state-of-the art helicopters, fighter planes, assault rifles, and other advanced technology, coupled with chemical weapons to defoliate the jungles and burn the countryside, plus an ever-growing number of young American men on the ground. Villagers trying to bring in their crops died along with the guerrilla fighters, their homes and communities destroyed by aerial bombings, toxic defoliants, and sometimes by ARVN and US troops who could not distinguish between neutral or sympathetic villagers and Viet Cong guerrillas.[17]

At home, especially for draft-age citizens, many began to question this undeclared war. The US military, virtually propping up the South Vietnamese government for years on end, lost the battle for "hearts and minds" in Vietnam and in the United States.[18] During Patterson's thirteen months in Vietnam, 118 American soldiers were killed in the conflict. The next year 206 American soldiers died in Vietnam. In 1968, the year of the Tet Offensive and the apex of US involvement in the war, 16,592 American soldiers died in the war. Even though the Tet Offensive was a military success for the United States and its allies, with the Viet Cong never really recovering from the heavy losses of this prolonged military action, a growing percentage of the American people had lost faith in the abilities and claims of their military and political leaders.[19]

When President John F. Kennedy was assassinated on November 22, 1963, Vice President Lyndon B. Johnson assumed the office of president on that same day. Winning the presidency in his own right in 1964, Johnson escalated the Vietnam War through the continuous urging of officials in the Pentagon and the Department of Defense. By 1968 the unpopularity of the war and his presidency were at such a level that he determined not to seek reelection, and the US participation in the Vietnam War became the fulcrum of the 1968 presidential election between Hubert H. Humphrey and Richard M. Nixon. Both candidates responded to a growing uproar over the capriciousness of the draft, the toll on a generation of young men, and basic issues concerning US military interventions to fight communism. While the United States did not completely extricate itself from the Vietnam War until 1973, the shift in policies and goals began with the election of Nixon in 1969. The United States sent almost a half million soldiers to Vietnam in 1968. Every year thereafter the numbers were less, in a concerted effort to extricate the nation from this war while somehow claiming victory.[20] If participation in the Vietnam War was a necessity, Patterson was fortunate to have had that experience early on in the conflict, and he believes it was important for him to have served, "because I'd never been around the world before." And he says, "It made you grow up quickly. You became a man overnight to survive."

Patterson remains philosophical about his time in a war zone and points to an exchange he had before shipping out to Vietnam. "A white fellow in AIT with me, he was from New York, Italian; he didn't like black folks. I said, 'Man if you needed some blood and my blood was okay, . . . you be thinking, 'I don't need your blood'? And it so happens he went to Vietnam. I didn't see it, but he had to have blood, and a black fellow gave him the blood. You see, you don't ever know who's going to bring you a cup of water. It behooves us to treat all humans fair."

Patterson's time in the service matured him. "It gave me a different perspective of what America was about," he says. "Go to a foreign place where you see communism in action. Your ideas will change."[21]

Patterson completed his service commitment in March 1963, and nothing could come close to the feeling he had when he returned to the "World," as American troops called the United States. "When I came back, I kissed Travis Air Force Base," Patterson says. "I was glad to get back home." As soon as possible, he returned to Lubbock and settled into a committed rhythm of work and family. In December of 1963, T. J. and Bobbie welcomed Shelia, their third child, into the family, and the Pattersons continued to build their lives around raising their small children and teaching. Patterson resumed his varied responsibilities at Mary and Mac Private School. Bobbie explains their routine: "I always worked at the schools," she says. "T. J. was still driving a bus. I stayed home and did subbing and got the kids to school."[22]

Looking back on their childhoods, the three Patterson children have strong memories of the close-knit family life they shared with their parents. Avis Elise, the oldest child and caretaker of her younger brother and sister, explains the core rules of the family. "Number one, respect your mother and father and your family. Your family was the main, most important thing," she says.

Avis is the quiet sibling. "Compared to my brother and sister, yes, I can be talkative," she says, "but I'm not as aggressive as they are." Avis remembers herself when a child as "an old woman in a young body." She often acted as the straw boss for her mother and father. "The funny thing about me is they really never had to ever get on to me about responsibilities around the house. It was already in me," she says. "I was the one that was always cleaning, fussing at the other two because they weren't doing their part. My mom would come home, and I'd have dinner ready. They never had any problem out of me in that respect."

Avis also shares her memories of her father as a very engaged parent and husband. "I actually watched him around the house. . . . I've always looked up to my father, and even as I got older, I used to say to myself that I wanted a husband just like him. He would cook around the house, and, actually, I used to watch him a lot, and he taught me how to cook. I'd see him clean the house. I'd see him go to the grocery store. I saw him with all types of hats on, and I just fell in love with him for who he was."[23]

Tommy Patterson remembers that his father's guidance extended beyond the Patterson family. "He was also concerned about the self-esteem of young people, T. J., Jr., says. " Always wanted to make sure that the young people knew they were somebody, wanted them to carry themselves as if they were somebody, holding their head high. Always teaching basics of becoming a young man; always shaking a man's hand firm and always tell them to look a man in the eye when you talk to him."[24]

Shelia insists that the years since her childhood have changed her father. "Wow. He's mellowed out a lot," she exclaims. "When we were young, my dad was fresh out of the military, and that's how he ran the home. It was 'Yes, sir. No, sir.'. . . And you sure weren't going to disrespect my mom!"

Shelia learned early that her father didn't mince words, and the Patterson children didn't try to test his resolve. "He told us when we were kids, and I remember this, that if we ever disrespected that lady, my mom, we'd have to leave Lubbock. . . . That stuck with me . . . not that we would anyway because my mom packed a pretty powerful punch herself. That was embedded in us, but of course, we weren't going to chance it."[25]

Spankings were also a basic part of their upbringing. Patterson addresses the issue. "The neighbor whipped my behind, then took me home. That's how I was raised, and it helped me," he says. "It helped me. It helped me, and I thank God for that because you don't ask a kid what they want to do all the time. You tell them what they'd better do. You don't debate with a child."[26]

Shelia remembers the possibilities of a whipping. "My dad didn't do so much. My dad could just speak and that was enough; but we did, we got our share. I think I got more than the other two," she adds. "I'm the baby, so I kind of tested the water a little bit more. But they didn't spare the rod."[27]

All three children admit that Bobbie was the parent who enforced the rules of the home. Tommy says, "Our mom was the strict disciplinarian. Our dad tried to be, but he was mostly talk. Our mom was all action. Dad was all talk, but he was such a big man that we feared him anyway—not fear but respect. He was bigger than we were, and if we were bad, we did get in big trouble."

According to Tommy, his father had tenderness for all his children, but his son thinks his dad was softer on the girls in the family. "He definitely had soft spots for us, my baby sister, most importantly. I was the middle child," he points out. "And, of course, my oldest sister, he always had a soft spot for her as well."[28]

Avis celebrates that relationship. "I hear a lot about daughters who never had a relationship with their fathers," she says. "So I felt very blessed to have my father in my home. Not only to have him in the same house as my mother, but also the relationship he and I had."[29]

Tommy says, "I always kid him. There was . . . a difference between little girls, little boys." But he notes emphatically, "He was a great father. He took time with us. He came to all my football games when I played youth-wide football games. When I played Eastern Little League baseball, he would try to be there most of the time. He got me active in Cub Scouts and Boy Scouts also. When I played basketball, back then it was called South Plains Boys Club, he was always there."[30]

In the Patterson home dinnertime rules were very basic. You didn't waste food. Shelia recalls an incident with her sister that has remained with her throughout the years. The family was about to enjoy a meal of homemade chili when Avis insisted that her chili be Frito pie. "All the rest of us were just going to eat chili," Shelia says. "We were satisfied with chili and crackers, however you dress it up, but my sister wanted Frito pie. So, my mom made my dad go to the store and get Fritos. . . . She wanted a big bowl of Frito pie, and we were like 'don't do it, don't do it.' . . . And Dad said, 'You want Frito pie, you're going to eat that Frito pie because you know we don't waste food.'" Avis attempted to consume her Texas-sized dinner, and Shelia shakes her head as she recalls, "I can still see my brother and I standing in the corner of the kitchen just laughing and going, "We told her.'"

Eventually, Patterson felt his point had been made and relented on making Avis finish her meal, but Shelia points out, "He was just back from Vietnam, and it had an impression on him, the fact that people were starving, children were begging, and all of that."

Shelia tells another story about the basics of the dinner table. "We had a cousin," she begins. "His name was Gary Wadley, and Gary was an only child. He was my mom's sister's son. He spent a lot of time with us, so people thought there were four children instead of just three. But the one big thing my dad taught was that you don't waste food. . . . After Vietnam he talked about the Viet Cong, and how he's seen children going hungry, so you did not waste food. . . . I remember specifically my cousin Gary threw a piece of bread in the trash. My dad said, 'Oh no!' and so what we had to do is we had to come out and split that. You may think that's harsh, but we don't waste. You don't throw stuff away. There are people across the country who are starving. It wasn't a filthy piece of bread. He wouldn't have done that, but it was to make a point. I don't think we had to finish it off, but we did. It was broke into four pieces and that was done to teach us all that none of us were going to waste."

Attending the Bethel AME Church on Sunday was another basic rule of the Patterson home. "As we got older," Shelia says, "he didn't care what time we came in on Saturday night, you were going to church on Sunday morning, wearing whatever you came in wearing the night before or whatever. You're going because he was the Sunday school superintendent. If there were no other children in Sunday school on Sunday morning, Avis, Shelia, and Tommy, and Gary because he was part of us too, we were there."[31]

The three Patterson children attended their great-aunt Lucille Graves's Mary and Mac Private School, participated in the Bethel AME Church, and joined in a home life full of clear lines of discipline and abounding affection. Bobbie and T. J. worked very hard at being strong and loving parents and engaging their family in the social dynamics of the Eastside. In 1965 Patterson extended his outreach to East Lubbock, when he applied for a job with the Community Action Board, the local arm of President

Lyndon B. Johnson's War on Poverty. He was hired as assistant director to Director Joe Kelly and later promoted to director of the Lubbock Office of Economic Opportunity (OEO), taking on the challenge of keeping the various new social programs of the times efficient and effective.

The Kennedy assassination was a deep and festering wound to the nation, and in taking up the mantle of the office, President Johnson pledged to support and carry out Kennedy's ambitious domestic programs on civil rights and poverty. With a landslide victory in his own presidential election in 1964, Johnson expanded on Kennedy's legislative agenda and named his sweeping domestic program the Great Society. Johnson was a masterful legislator, and through his well-honed talents for arm-twisting and horse-trading, he succeeded in passing over 200 bills aimed at changing the fabric of the nation. Among other things the Johnson administration established Medicare and Medicaid to ensure health care for the poor and elderly, increased Social Security benefits, expanded the federal food stamp program, and implemented a series of federal consumer protection policies.

Johnson responded to the persistent and violent conflict over civil rights by successfully passing two signature pieces of legislation. The Civil Rights Act of 1964 forbade job discrimination against minorities and women and the segregation of public accommodations. The Voting Rights Act of 1965 assured minorities the right to register and vote, with a monitoring system put in place to stand vigil over the process.

Kennedy had created a series of task forces to study the complex issues of poverty in America and succeeded in passing significant legislation during his brief tenure, but many other legislative efforts had stalled in Congress. Johnson revived these bills and expanded upon them, proclaiming at Ohio University on May 7, 1964, an "unconditional war on poverty," where, he said, "no child will go unfed, and no youngster will go unschooled." The Economic Opportunity Act of 1964 created the Office of Economic Opportunity (OEO) to oversee a number of community-based antipoverty programs framed and implemented at the local level. Along with William A. Mullins, Kennedy's brother-in-law Sargent Shriver, of Peace Corp fame, became the architect of the War on Poverty and served as its first director.[32]

As the local director of the Office of Economic Opportunity (OEO), Patterson was charged with organizing and implementing a battery of promising new opportunities for poor Hispanic, black, and white people in Lubbock County. The OEO established the Job Corps to help disadvantaged youth develop marketable skills; VISTA to recruit volunteers to teach and empower the poor; the Model Cities Program to support urban development; Upward Bound to assist high school students prepare for college; the Community Action Program to help the poor become self-sufficient; and Project Head Start, offering preschool education to poor children.

Patterson had a great admiration for Director Shriver and the VISTA program he had fashioned on the Peace Corps model for problem solving here at home. Patterson coordinated a summer jobs program for young people who were charged with picking up trash in local parks for $1.50 an hour, with headquarters at the Mae Simmons Party House and East Tenth Street, across from Posey Elementary. He also found his work with Head Start very gratifying. Head Start is often touted as the most successful of the War on Poverty programs. Originally established as an eight-week summer program for poor children, it was quickly expanded to offer preschool to vulnerable children all year long.[33] Patterson coordinated an outreach program between the city of Lubbock and Head Start to address a series of community health needs, including tests for sickle cell anemia, high blood pressure, malnutrition, and other physical vulnerabilities. He says of the OEO, "I thought it was a great thing!" and believes the local OEO community action boards held great promise for the five Head Start centers in Lubbock, Slaton, Roosevelt, Shallowater, and New Deal, advising and administering on matters such as economics, childcare, health, and legal issues.

The War on Poverty represented a new level of federal engagement in the local community, and these opportunities were often met with suspicion and reaction from local officials, especially in an isolated place like Lubbock, with a mixed record of responding to the needs of the poor and minority populations. Washington, the Lubbock County Commissioners Court, and the Lubbock City Council all had a hand in the operation. Because the programs were brand new, with a federal component, Patterson's task required patience and skill in coordinating the funds for implementation. He was challenged by mounds of paperwork for accountability and layers of officials to appease and cajole. He explains the problem: "Someone had to come to the regional office and stand on the courthouse steps, and say, 'May I fund you for the next fiscal year?'"

He remembers the challenges he faced trying to provide the community with these new tools for fighting poverty. "Ever hear of Al Couch?" Patterson asks. "He was director of personnel and a bad dude at City Hall.

We could not ask him for nothing. Could not use the facilities. Could not have an office in the building, but they utilized our money—the city and the county. Why can't we have an office there? The only place for us was on Nineteenth Street, the federal building. But it was not a federal program locally. It was called community action, not federal action. It was a local program. It was called the community action board, with about forty regional board members locally. But you could not have an office space in City Hall."[34]

Patterson served as Lubbock County OEO director from 1965 to 1972, and during that time he expanded his contacts and his voice within East Lubbock and the community at large. He was in a position to improve conditions, and he did. He was in a position to learn the skills to negotiate with conflicting factions, and he did. He stood as the local representative for a new pathway to improving the lives of the poor, but from the beginning the War on Poverty was beset by problems, a large number just in the nature of such a sweeping effort to bring about intrinsic change to the structure of community. The Vietnam War soon became another problem when, more and more, the financial resources of the nation found their way to the jungles of Southeast Asia rather than Main Street.

In spite of it all, however, the Great Society helped bring about revolutionary changes to the country. In 1960, 55 percent of African Americans lived below the poverty line, and by 1968 the percentage had dropped to 27 percent. VISTA continues today as AmeriCorps VISTA, with 7,000 members serving in over 1,000 projects throughout the nation. Head Start remains a vital and successful preschool resource for poor children throughout the nation. Medicaid and Medicare have remained a crucial part of the health care system, improving the health of vulnerable children and retirement-age citizens for the past fifty years. The Civil Rights Act and the Voting Rights Act, coupled with the 1966 repeal of the poll tax, have given black citizens, as well as other minorities, a dynamic role in the politics of the nation, leading to the election of minority representatives and senators, and in 2008 and again in 2012, the election of Barack Hussein Obama, the first black president of the United States.[35]

The changes influenced by Great Society legislation became apparent almost immediately, not simply in infrastructure programs but in social and racial attitudes. Patterson's story is a notable example. In 1972 Dean Jack Steele of the Texas Tech University College of Business Administration offered T. J. Patterson a position as assistant dean of the college to help guide freshmen students and teach core courses in business administration. This administrative offer came from the very institution of higher education that had refused Patterson's enrollment as a graduate student in 1959 solely because of the color of his skin.

Chapter 4

"And the Walls Came Tumbling Down"

Patterson has always believed he was drafted because of his efforts to enroll in graduate school at Texas Technological College when the school was still a whites-only institution. While the claim seems rather far-fetched from a distant vantage point, there is little doubt that throughout the 1960s the Vietnam War draft was a capricious affair. Local draft boards chose who was selected to serve, and these local boards were made up of community leaders easily influenced by the mothers, fathers, and draft-age young men they knew. Few were eager to embrace the call, and as the war escalated, the way people were chosen for active duty became a volatile public issue. Draft exemptions included full-time college enrollment, service in the Peace Corps, and marriage with children. The complete list of deferments left poor, single, white and minority men to fight the war at an average age of nineteen.[1] From 1961 to 1966, African Americans accounted for almost 20 percent of all combat deaths in Vietnam, even though they were only 11 percent of the population,[2] and Martin Luther King decried this circumstance in a 1967 speech given at Riverside Church in New York City. Criticizing the diversion of monies from domestic programs to the war effort, King said, "We were taking the black young men who had been crippled by our society and sending them eight thousand miles away to guarantee liberties in Southeast Asia which they had not found in Southwest Georgia and East Harlem."[3]

Patterson's military service came some years before the Vietnam draft turned into an overt issue of race and privilege, but that he was drafted despite the fact that he was married with two babies does raise suspicions that something must have been amiss for this most basic deferment to be ignored. Patterson believes his exchange with Texas Tech President R. C. Goodwin had something to do with it.

In 1959, a year after he arrived in Lubbock, Patterson made a visit to the Texas Technological College campus, located just on the west edge of downtown, to inquire about enrollment procedures for entering graduate school. He was promptly escorted out of the building. That President Goodwin refused to see him in his office has remained a bitter memory. "Dr. Goodwin wouldn't talk to me inside the Administration Building. He came outside," Patterson says. "I had to go outside to talk to him."

Once on the grounds, Goodwin explained why he couldn't accept his application. Patterson remembers the conversation vividly. "He said, 'T. J., you know I can't let you in,' and he showed me the catalog. The little red, black, and white booklet stated, 'This shall be known as the Texas Technological College and only white students shall attend.'" Patterson remembers his indignant response. "'Dr. Goodwin, one day,' I said, 'one day, we are going to go to school here.'"[4] In 1959 it was a rare circumstance for a lone black man to challenge the word of any white man, let alone a college president, but Patterson's retort would soon ring true.

That "one day" arrived two years later, in the summer of 1961, when Patterson's Aunt Lucille Sugar Barton Graves was admitted to the graduate school of Texas Technological College. Graves, already armed with her bachelor's degree, had spent the past six months trying to enroll in the only institution of higher education offering graduate courses in Lubbock. Since 1955 she had built her private school from a small preschool startup into an Eastside institution, offering kindergarten classes through high-school diploma. She had also become a dynamic part of the Texas African American educator network and was determined to enhance her credentials while she served as chief administrator of the Mary and Mac Private School. Patterson says of his aunt, "She owned the school. She was independent. You couldn't frighten her."[5] Frustrated with the continual admission refusals from Texas Tech, Graves contacted the Dallas chapter of the NAACP for help, and the organization planned to file a discrimination suit against the college a week after the deadline for summer enrollment. Graves told President Goodwin she had made an appeal to the NAACP. In the last hour of the last day of the second summer session enrollment, Goodwin contacted Graves and told her if she could get to Texas Tech in fifteen minutes, she could enroll.[6]

Too nervous to drive, Graves enlisted the help of a friend to take her to the campus. They made it in time, and Graves gained admission for the second summer semester of 1961, becoming the first African American to enter Texas Technological College and blazing the trail for a number of other black students to enter that fall. Besides his high-handed way of accepting the defeat of an unlawful admissions policy, many have speculated that Goodwin's eleventh-hour permission for Graves to enroll was a gambit to keep her admission out of the eye of the local press and segregationist members of the Texas Tech board of regents.[7]

In a 1982 article in the *Southwest Digest*, Graves comments on her first semester at Texas Tech. "I took two classes," she says. "In one class, there were twenty-seven whites and one black—me. The professors wouldn't speak to you. The atmosphere was so heavy you could cut it."[8] In spite of classroom tension, her efforts brought about the integration of Texas Tech without further incident, and Graves went on to receive a doctorate of humanities from the University of Houston while continuing her career as administrator of the Mary and Mac Private School until her retirement in 1991.[9]

By 1961 the NAACP had become such an effective legal force for public-school integration, it sometimes only took the suggestion of filing an NAACP discrimination suit to persuade a segregated institution to finally relent, especially since the *Brown* ruling of 1954 and the *Brown II* ruling of 1955 left little room for argument over the necessity to integrate public institutions. Virgil Johnson says that he, his wife, Ida Johnson, and T. J. Patterson were planning on filing a case of their own against the Texas Tech whites-only enrollment policy when Graves' successful admission rendered the issue moot.[10] *Brown v. Board of Education* made the doctrine of "separate but equal" illegal in public education. In the preceding twenty years, the NAACP had been vigorously litigating cases using the "separate but equal" principle of *Plessy v. Ferguson* against itself, gradually building a body of successful court cases that revealed the conspicuous lack of equality in black education. These legal efforts ultimately led to the *Brown* decision, which struck at the core of a racially segregated nation.

Often called the "Moses of the civil-rights movement," Charles Hamilton Houston was the long-serving dean of Howard University Law School when in 1935 he was appointed as the first special counsel of the NAACP. In that role he developed the legal strategy to chip away at "separate but equal." Basing his battle plan around Nathan Margold's observation that facilities for blacks were always separate but never equal, Houston focused NAACP court cases on the equal requirement of *Plessy v. Ferguson* and filed a series of lawsuits demanding that black educational facilities and white educational facilities in a state be equivalent. The public-education system was the broad target of his "equalization strategy," and Houston often chose to challenge whites-only law schools, recognizing that states could rarely afford to offer equal professional schools, one for whites and one for blacks, and that judges would immediately understand the qualitative differences of separate law schools, if indeed they existed. Through NAACP court challenges, the University of Maryland School of Law was integrated in 1936 and the University of Missouri School of Law in 1938.[11]

In 1939 Thurgood Marshall succeeded his mentor Houston as NAACP special counsel and in 1940 founded the NAACP Legal Defense Fund, generating the financial support and a seasoned team of lawyers to challenge "separate but equal" in every corner of the land. In 1946 Thurgood Marshall came to Texas to join Texas NAACP attorneys in arguing a case for Heman Marion Sweatt. Sweatt was a Wiley College graduate who wanted to attend law school and was initially advised by famous Texas civil-rights lawyer William J. Durham to apply to the strictly segregated University of Texas Law School and challenge the institution's racial policies. When he was denied admission because he was black, the NAACP filed suit. At that time there was no law school in Texas that accepted black students, but when the NAACP filed *Sweatt v. Painter*, Texas leaders quickly scrambled to create one. The Travis County district court issued a six-month continuance of the case to give the state legislature time to pass Texas State Senate Bill 140 and create a law school in the brand new Texas State University for Negroes, established on June 14, 1947, in Houston. Texas courts ruled that these accommodations satisfied the requirements of "separate but equal," but the NAACP challenged the decision through the federal appeals process, with Thurgood Marshall finally arguing the case before the US Supreme Court in 1950. The Supreme Court reversed the Texas courts, ruling that the University of Texas Law School and the Texas State University for Negroes Law School were definitely not equal.

In *Sweatt v. Painter* the Supreme Court decision included a list of glaring inequalities between the white and black facilities: "The University of Texas Law School had 16 full-time and 3 part-time professors, while the black law school had 5 full-time professors. The University of Texas Law School had 850 students and a law library of 65,000 volumes, while the black law school had 23 students and a library of 16,500 volumes. The University of Texas Law School had moot court facilities, an Order of the Coif affiliation, and numerous graduates involved in public and private law practice, while the black law school had only one practice court facility and only one graduate admitted to the Texas Bar." Heman Marion Sweatt entered the University of Texas School of Law as the first black student in the fall of 1950 and effectively integrated the University of Texas Graduate School. Today, the Travis County courthouse in Austin, Texas, has been renamed the Heman Sweatt Courthouse.[12]

The NAACP filed another interesting Texas lawsuit in 1951. Patterson was in ninth grade when Willie Faye Battle applied for admission to Harden Junior College, part of the newly constituted Midwestern University in Wichita Falls, Texas. Battle was valedictorian of the class of 1950 from the local black high school, Booker T. Washington, and was denied admission to Harden Junior College because of her race. After numerous efforts by the local African American community and consistent rejection of their appeals by the Midwestern University board of regents, the NAACP Legal Defense Fund in Dallas filed a discrimination case against the school, pointing out that Harden Junior College as part of Midwestern University was the only local public institution of higher learning available to the citizens of Wichita Falls. In this case, there was no semblance of separate or equal for black students in their hometown.

Usually NAACP discrimination suits in the early 1950s were denied at the state level, then proceeded through the appeals process, ending up at the US Supreme Court, where Marshall and his team of lawyers argued separate-but-not-equal cases on a regular basis. However, in *Battle et al. v. Wichita Falls Junior College District et al.*, North Texas District Judge William H. Atwell handed down a ruling for the plaintiff right from the start, in spite of the Texas attorney general's filing an *amicus curiae* on behalf of the state of Texas supporting segregation in public education.[13]

Judge Atwell had been appointed as district judge by President Warren G. Harding in 1923 and was a crusty character who had compromised his political career by speaking out against the Texas Ku Klux Klan in the 1920s and later criticized the US Supreme Court over civil rights, asserting from the bench that the 1954 *Brown* decision had been "based on sociological opinion rather than law."[14] He was deeply committed to the strict letter of the law, and on November 27, 1951, Atwell handed down his decision ordering Midwestern University to integrate because the institution had not fulfilled its obligation to provide separate and equal educational opportunities for the black community of Wichita Falls. Midwestern received a stay on Atwell's orders with an appeal to the Fifth Circuit Court of Appeals in New Orleans. In May of 1953, the Fifth Circuit ruled unanimously to uphold Atwell's decision. Midwestern applied for a rehearing and was denied, then appealed to the US Supreme Court and was placed on the docket, creating another automatic stay of Atwell's integration ruling.

On May 17, 1954, *Brown v. Board of Education of Topeka* was handed down, and the US Supreme Court rejected the appeal for *Battle et al. v. Wichita Falls Junior College District et al.* as already decided by *Brown*, letting Atwell's 1951 integration order stand. In the fall semester of 1954, at the very time that T. J. Patterson was entering his freshman year at Bishop College, twelve black students were accepted to Midwestern University.[15] Patterson remembers this court case from his high-school years and was aware that Harden Junior College as part of Midwestern University had become a genuine possibility for his own undergraduate education, a possibility his stepfather encouraged. However, Bishop College boasted a long and proud history of black education, and he had been offered a scholarship. It was very gratifying to receive support from the school, albeit meager support, and besides, he says, "I was ready to get out of town."[16]

In 1972 the fact that Patterson was offered the position of assistant dean of the Texas Tech College of Business Administration is a significant indication of how much the racial fabric of higher education had changed since the days of *Sweatt, Battle*, and Patterson's own 1959 rejection by President Goodwin. The violent conflicts that accompanied the integration of higher education in the South had subsided. James Meredith was admitted to the University of Mississippi in 1962 as the first black student attending that institution, in spite of the antagonism of Governor Ross Barnett and mob rule throughout the college town of Oxford. Even with Governor George Wallace pledging to "stand at the schoolhouse door" in defiance of federal troops, integration prevailed at the University of Alabama, with two black students gaining admission in 1963, leaving Wallace to rail against the federal government as a candidate for US president in 1964 and 1968. In Texas black undergraduates were admitted to the University of Texas in 1956, after the US Supreme Court enjoined all public institutions of higher education to integrate "with all deliberate speed." Texas A&M admitted a black student to its Arlington State College campus in 1962 and accepted five black students into the A&M Corps of Cadets after passage of the Civil Rights Act in 1964.[17] By 1972 federal mandates were solidly in place, and institutions of higher learning were beginning to embrace a new sensibility to racial diversity in both the classroom and college athletics.

Patterson joined the administrative team of Dean Jack Steele to work primarily with freshman students in a business college that boasted the second-largest enrollment in the nation. He taught two sections of an introductory class in business basics to prepare college majors for the core curriculum of accounting, finance, marketing, management information systems (MIS), and discipline. His classes met on Tuesdays and Thursdays at 9:00 a.m. and at 11:00 a.m., with 405 students in each section. He valued the exchange. "I had all kinds of kids that would talk to me, and I enjoyed that," he says. "We had all kinds of personalities—lots of elite and highly visible students, even the governor of Texas' daughter was in my class."

While many of Patterson's students were from wealthy, well-known Texas families, one of his most notorious students was John Hinckley, the young man who shot President Ronald Reagan in 1981, trying to impress teenage movie actress, Jodie Foster. Patterson remembers him as a quiet student and says of him, "I didn't know him personally. He was a barefooted, rich, white boy." The contrast between the quiet, affluent hippie in his classroom and the attempted assassin that Hinckley became has remained a puzzle. "How could such a quiet fellow do what he did? I couldn't understand it," Patterson admits. "Sometimes you can be filled up inside, and it has to come out."

Texas Tech did not experience the student unrest that characterized the spirit of many other campuses during these times of protest marches against the Vietnam War, racial injustice, and women's inequality. Nevertheless, Texas Tech students did assume the trappings of the protest culture, sporting long hair, beards, sandals, and vibrantly colored theatrical costumes. Patterson was amused by the scene. "These white kids would come to Lubbock and become hippies, no haircuts, nothing. By the time they go back home, they clean up. I said, 'Where did y'all go with your bad-acting selves?'" In spite of their rather hypocritical showmanship, Patterson appreciated his classroom charges. "Kids!" he says. "Young people was just young people. They were outstanding young people. I enjoyed them."[18]

In 1978, in addition to his teaching obligations, Patterson was awarded a commission in the US Navy signed by President Jimmy Carter. He served six years as a campus liaison officer in a program aimed at increasing minority recruitment in the ROTC officer program. He was based at Texas Tech with headquarters in Albuquerque, New Mexico, and traveled to navy bases in San Diego, California, and Norfolk, Virginia. In 1984 Patterson was promoted to commander before resigning the Navy commission to run for office.

While Patterson pursued a career in government service and higher education, Bobbie Patterson followed a very successful professional pathway in public-school education. After teaching in Ralls, then Plainview, Texas, she settled into elementary-school teaching on the Eastside at Hunt Elementary, Wheatley Elementary, and Parkway Elementary, experiencing firsthand the challenges and accomplishments of the Lubbock Independent School District (LISD) desegregation process.

The year after the *Brown* decision, the LISD school board quietly adopted a new school policy, stating that "beginning in 1955–56 no distinction in the various schools of the Lubbock public schools in pupil attendance shall be made by reason of race or color."[19] This new integration policy was really just for the books. It went virtually unnoticed by the press and the people because public-school attendance was based on residential neighborhoods, and Lubbock neighborhoods were strictly defined by color. A federal study released in 1960 named Lubbock as "the fourth-most residentially segregated city of the central Southwest."[20] African Americans, numbering 12,459 in the 1960 census, lived in the area of town bordered, north to south, by Fourth Street and Thirty-fourth Street and, west to east, by Avenue C and Loop 289, then just barely under construction. At the same time Lubbock Hispanics numbered 17,003 and were relegated to the isolated neighborhood of Guadalupe, bordered, north to south, by Yellowhouse Canyon and Fourth Street and, west to east, by Avenue Q and Avenue H, or what is now Buddy Holly Avenue. The rest of Lubbock was decidedly white, numbering around 120,000 people who lived south and west of downtown.[21]

There was very little racial or cultural comingling of any kind, a circumstance Patterson noticed when he arrived in town and instinctively knew was a political mistake, diminishing the voices of both African Americans and Hispanics. "This was crazy," he says. "Thousands of Hispanics on Broadway, thousands of blacks on Avenue A, but they never came together—ever!"[22] Actually, Hispanics gathered downtown only on the east edge of Broadway, as Robert Narvaiz points out. "I remember when I first came to Lubbock, Avenue H [Buddy Holly Avenue] was about as far as we could go. If we went beyond Avenue H, we couldn't go into those stores. I went into the service in 1958 and got out in 1962, and when I got back to Lubbock, I found that everything was still about the same. I remember thinking that I went into the service to fight for my country and then get back home and had to fight again."[23] Only bootleggers, prostitutes, and other people living on the far edge of the law crossed the rigid racial lines that defined the Lubbock community, and Patterson recognized the importance of overcoming this ethnic separation from the very start.

When he was elected to the Lubbock city council in 1984, Patterson quickly established a dynamic working relationship with newly elected District 1 councilwoman Maggie Trejo. Together they built meaningful coalitions in support of programs benefiting the traditional black and Hispanic neighborhoods, and Patterson continued his strong advocacy of a broad-based minority coalition. "Blacks and brown in Lubbock must learn to stick together," he says. "That's so key and crucial. If they know whence they come from in this town, they cannot afford to go the opposite direction. Forget about who has the largest number."[24]

It was through the gradual change in public school policies that the tripartite racial segregation of Lubbock began to ease. In 1965 the LISD school board approved the integration of the district teaching staff, and a glimmer of ethnic crossover began, but the schools remained products of the surrounding neighborhoods, and the children attending were all of one color, all black, all brown, or all white. In 1970 the US Justice Department took note, alleging that federal financial assistance funds were "administered in a racially discriminatory manner, or would support a program infected by a racially discriminating environment."[25] The US government brought suit against the Lubbock Independent School District, and it fell to US Senior District Judge Halbert O. Woodward to oversee LISD efforts to meet the demands of the Justice Department.

Unlike the Lubbock city council at-large election system that suffered from a tradition of white businessman inbreeding, the at-large system of the LISD school board had some success in electing minorities. In 1970 Joan Ervin was elected to fill an open LISD school board position and holds the distinction of being the first African American elected to office in Lubbock. She was reelected in 1972, and in 1985 Hispanic restaurateur Jose Ramirez was also elected to the LISD school board under the at-large system.[26]

Joan Ervin served on the school board during the initial LISD desegregation plan that targeted for integration the four Eastside schools of Dunbar High School, Struggs Junior High, Iles Elementary, and Wheatley Elementary. In the 1970–71 school year Dunbar was integrated, with 263 Anglo and 82 Hispanic students bused to the school. The school remained open and officially integrated, despite the fact that a white student shot a black student on the Dunbar campus that year, followed by an uproar in the black community and the shooting of a policeman. The incident was downplayed in the press and has been rarely spoken of since.[27] Struggs ninth-graders were transferred to other schools. These cursory efforts, however, did not remedy the situation, and the LISD school board spent the next twenty-one years grappling with an acceptable integration system for the Lubbock public schools. At one point, after a 1978 court order, LISD was busing 2,000 students daily to meet Judge Woodward's desegregation requirements.[28]

In 1985 Bidal Aguero, owner of the Hispanic newspaper *El Editor*, along with three others, filed a lawsuit to change LISD school board elections to a single-member system. The issue was resolved out of court, establishing a new policy that five members be elected from single-member districts and two on an at-large basis. E. C. Leslie, LISD superintendent in 1985, admitted that the protracted discrimination case against the district convinced the LISD school board to settle and avoid the cost and time of another court battle.[29]

Bobbie Patterson was in the middle of her elementary-teaching career when the fits and starts of public-school integration began to change the complexion of Eastside classrooms. She was present to welcome ever-changing groups of white students to the classroom in the rotational dance of the races created by the busing patterns of the times. In spite of these district-wide integration dynamics, Avis Patterson and Tommy Patterson managed to follow a family tradition of education that had begun at Aunt Lucille Graves's Mary and Mac Private School. They then both attended their neighborhood schools of Iles Elementary, Struggs Junior High, and Dunbar High School. Avis was head cheerleader and Miss Black Lubbock in 1977, the year she graduated and enrolled at Texas Tech. Tommy graduated in 1979, then left town to attend North Texas State University in Denton. Shelia was the only Patterson sibling who got caught up directly in the LISD integration experiment. She began her education at Mary and Mac Private School, then attended Iles Elementary, but Struggs Junior High offered only seventh and eighth grades when she arrived. For ninth grade, Shelia was bused out of the Eastside to O. L. Slaton Junior High on Avenue Q and Thirty-second Street, returning the next year to attend Dunbar High School. She graduated in 1981 from Dunbar Struggs High School, renamed following the closing of Struggs Junior High School.

Shelia attended public school right in the middle of the topsy-turvy attempts at meaningful integration and observes, "At Iles, the only way our schools integrated was our teachers were white. All the students were black, and we had a handful of Hispanics, and I don't recall any white students. My junior year they started, in the name of desegregation, . . . allowing the students, the minority students, to go to other schools. . . . All the vocational students, they had the choice of continuing at their home school or coming over to Dunbar. . . . The school was integrated but at noon, when all the students went to finish their day, it was back to status quo."[30] The vocational program was only for a half day.

Besides the cultural whirlwind caused by the 1970 desegregation suit, on May 11 of that same year, Lubbock was hit by a category F5 tornado. The tornado slashed a devastating path one and a half miles wide and eight miles long through downtown Lubbock, the Guadalupe neighborhood, and the Lubbock Country Club area. Guadalupe was turned to rubble, with only Saint Joseph's Catholic Church left standing. Many from this close-knit, lone Hispanic neighborhood were left homeless and given rent-free housing for a year in a Parkway neighborhood federal housing project, just north of the traditional Lubbock black community. Many other Hispanics moved to Arnett-Benson and North Overton. Still others received disaster relief to rebuild in Guadalupe, changing what had been the site of one of the largest substandard 1940s migrant worker camps into a cozy, middle-class neighborhood, Atzlan Park.[31]

The tornado dispersed the Lubbock Hispanic community into some predominantly white and some predominantly black areas of town, and this natural disaster, coupled with the desegregation order, brought the black and Hispanic communities closer together. By 1980 the great separation of the races had begun to slowly subside, and the comfort zone between the minorities that Patterson had wished for had begun to develop. Hispanic students were now joining black students at Dunbar, and Shelia remembers, "The students were pretty close because we went from junior high all the way through. Most of those students, the black students, came from Iles and Wheatley; the Spanish students came from Chris Harwell and Southeast."

Under the LISD integration experiment that offered students a choice of schools for certain courses, Shelia ventured out to attend Coronado High School in what was then the far-western retail area of central Lubbock. "I used to like to try things just because I liked to be different and challenging," she says. "I was, like, 'Well, shoot, if they can come to us, then I ought to be able to go over there.' So I took one class at Coronado, just for the heck of it, just because they said that I could. I took debate, and I did that just for the heck of it. But, in doing so, it kind of brought me in contact with a lot of people going 'what the heck do you think you're doing?'"

When Shelia returned to Dunbar, she kept up her interest in forensics. "I was on the speech team at Dunbar, and we did different tournaments and things like that. I did poetry and one-act. . . . One year, I was the only speech team member. If you pull the annual, it'll show 'Dunbar Speech Team, Shelia Patterson.'"

As indicated by people's reaction to Shelia's presence at Coronado High School, the growing interactions between blacks and Hispanics did not really extend into the predominantly white areas of Lubbock. By the 1970s minorities could enter retail stores in the broader community but not without suspicion from the clerks. Shelia recalls the looks as she shopped and vividly remembers an incident riding with a friend in central Lubbock. "When I was in high school, we had a day, it was called Twerp week where the girl asked the guy. There was a Hispanic guy. He didn't look Hispanic, but we were pretty good friends and I . . . had a little crush on him. So, I asked him. He came. He picked me up. We were driving down Nineteenth Street. There were some men that drove by us and threw bottles at the car because I was in the car with him."[32]

In 1978 the Lubbock desegregation challenge slowly began to find a meaningful solution through a magnet school concept. Iles Elementary became the first magnet school. From kindergarten through sixth grade, white children were bused in to participate in an open-concept educational experience, spearheaded by Dean Robert Anderson of the Texas Tech University College of Education and implemented by his wife, Linda Anderson, who served as an exemplary school principal. Soon, Iles Elementary had a long waiting list, and the dynamic educational environment created by the school served as a guide for minority-majority magnets and majority-minority magnets throughout the town. The Lubbock magnet school program implemented throughout specific elementary, junior high, and high schools, offered special courses and a special commitment to student diversity that finally led to the end of the long and arduous LISD desegregation suit.

In 1991 Judge Halbert O. Woodward declared the Lubbock Independent school system successfully integrated, allowing the district to operate its own affairs. To achieve this new freedom, the Lubbock public-school administration pledged to build Cavazos Junior High School on North University Avenue to respond to the growing student population in north Lubbock and expand the magnet program at Estacado High School to include medical and law enforcement courses.[33] Estacado High School is located on the Eastside, off what was then Quirt Avenue, a hauntingly symbolic name for an Eastside street since, according to Merriam-Webster, a "quirt" is "a riding whip with a short handle and a rawhide lash." When Patterson joined the Lubbock city council, he was instrumental in getting the name of this main artery through East Lubbock changed to Martin Luther King, Jr., Boulevard. The final agreement in the twenty-one-year desegregation case brought relief to all, accompanied by some outrage and great sorrow to the black community. As part of the final desegregation agreement, Dunbar Struggs High School was closed. Starting in 1993 all Eastside students would attend high school at the newer and larger Estacado, and Dunbar would become a junior high.

Patterson's dear friend Virgil Johnson was the principal of Dunbar Struggs when it closed as a high school. He remained as the principal of the newly constituted junior high but led a community vigil at the school to mourn its closing as the beacon of the black community, the traditional public gathering place for the Eastside. Years later, in a 2009 *Avalanche-Journal* article, Johnson says, "I still feel bad about it closing. . . . It was a great school, and it was such a part of the community and part of the city and part of the history of Lubbock, Texas, that I hated to see it close."[34]

Since the 1930s Dunbar High School had served as the pulse beat of the black community. Named for the black poet Paul Lawrence Dunbar, the first brick structure was built in 1936, becoming Iles Elementary in 1958 when a new and improved Dunbar High School was constructed in Manhattan Heights at East Twenty-sixth Street and Quirt Avenue. Three generations of community memories are wrapped up in that high school, and many prominent Lubbock black leaders have eagerly shared their reminiscences of the Dunbar High School experience.

Deputy City Manager Quincy White was a 1965 Dunbar graduate and says, "It was a real special place. . . . In the 1950s and 1960s, there were not a lot of options for black college graduates, so many of them became educators. . . . At Dunbar we had the cream of the crop in the classroom." White notes that the administrators and teachers treated students like their own children. Jackie Porch, past superintendent of the Lubbock State School and a 1969 Dunbar graduate, echoes his observation. "The teachers, the counselors, the principals, all of us lived in the same community. . . . There was a sense of community and of family. Any time you got in trouble, you couldn't get away because the principal lived across the street from you."

Vernita Woods-Holmes graduated from Dunbar in 1957 and served on the LISD school board from 2000 to 2016. She celebrates the school with a similar sense of longing and respect. "Right across the street from me was my principal and my first-grade teacher," she says. "My teachers were friends of my family, and a couple of my teachers were relatives. It was such a close-knit community."[35]

Dr. E. C. Struggs was the iconic principal of Dunbar, serving the school from 1930 until he retired in 1965. Under his strong leadership Dunbar became a four-year high school in 1932, ending the policy of only offering courses through eleventh grade to black students. An early black settler, Will Sedberry, explains with pride that he and his siblings all had high school educations "but we had to go all the way to Houston to get them due to the segregated nature [in Lubbock]."[36] Struggs changed all that and built an award-winning marching band, choir, and athletic program. The Dunbar Panthers basketball team won five state titles between 1953 and 1965, playing in the black Prairie View Interscholastic League.[37] The story of the Dunbar basketball team represents all that was lost and gained with integration and Patterson's constant efforts to bring East Lubbock and West Lubbock closer together.

The 1965 Dunbar state championship was coached by Curtis Gibson, who played in the 1953 state championship. The 1965 game and its outstanding players still inspire rich memories from those who played and those who drove these very tall young men, packed into two station wagons, 475 miles to Prairie View for the winning event. School buses were not available for that trek, and the *Avalanche-Journal* didn't cover that game or any other played by the Panthers in those days. They were never a part of the local athletic beat, and Dunbar athletic feats are still often left out of the winning statistics reported in the local media. Before integration Dunbar High School was totally cut off from the rest of the local public-school system. Quincy White tells a sports story to illustrate the point. He says that his wife "heard a former Monterey coach talking about a mile relay team he had back in the days of segregation. They had the fastest time in Texas. Someone suggested he go to Dunbar to practice against the Panthers. As the story goes, he found out his team wasn't even the fastest in Lubbock."

In 2010 Estacado High School won the state basketball title, appropriately assuming the mantel of athletic prowess inherited from its Dunbar roots. That championship was covered by the *Avalanche-Journal* with great enthusiasm. In the article the newspaper even acknowledged the

1965 Dunbar championship. The Lubbock Independent school system is also striving to acknowledge Dunbar High School achievements as part of Lubbock's "athletic footprint." When Mark Bell was LISD athletic director from 2010 to 2016, he began the task of trying to correct the record. "I worked extremely hard and long creating the LISD Hall of Honor," he says, "and made a point that Dunbar have a voice and representation in that organization. We have members in our inaugural class from Dunbar."[38]

This recent recognition of past athletic achievements by segregated black teams is an encouraging indication of a growing community respect for talent regardless of race or culture, and that inclusive community sensibility applies to overcoming other vestiges of segregation as well. In 2006 many were stunned to learn of the 1923 city ordinance that relegated African Americans to what became the Flats, south of Sixteenth Street and east of Avenue C. While the ordinance had been long forgotten as a real estate policy, it was still part of the city archives, and with appropriate expressions of outrage, the sitting 2006 Lubbock city council unanimously expunged the ordinance from the record.[39] Even then, many were shocked that it had taken over eighty years to formally repeal an ordinance that had served as a racial residential and commercial guideline for decades. In a 2016 online article entitled, "Wounds That Didn't Heal: Segregation in Lubbock," the author observes, "It's almost unimaginable that such an ordinance not only existed in the first place, but wasn't completely done away with until the 21st century."[40] Slowly but surely the racial and cultural walls of Lubbock are, indeed, crumbling, due in large part to the public-school desegregation process.

In 1999 *Avalanche-Journal* reporter Hank Murphy wrote a retrospective on the prolonged desegregation case, stating, "Some former Lubbock school officials have complained that the federal government used the schools to try to force integration on society as a whole." In response, LISD Superintendent Curtis Culwell countered, "I think that desegregation and court orders, in particular, were needed. The intervention was necessary to address inequalities in funding and resources that accompanied the concept of separate but equal schools."[41]

During the 2009 centennial celebration of Lubbock, the *Avalanche-Journal* contributed another retrospective on the desegregation case, with interviews of current LISD leaders and those who had struggled with the challenges of the suit directly. US Senior District Judge Halbert O. Woodward came in for much praise for his deft handling of the case throughout its twenty-one-year history. "I think we were fortunate to have a man as skilled and wise as Judge Woodward," says Wayne Havens, 2009 LISD superintendent and coach at Thompson and Smylie Wilson Junior High Schools in the early days of the case. "He took care of the district as a whole, and the decisions he made were made in the best interests of the kids." Havens also remembers the impact of the case as a parent. "At that time," he says, "I think the whole community was probably a little apprehensive. Once we got involved with it, though, it produced some of the best experiences our two boys had."

Former Lubbock school board member and Texas State school board member Donald Craig was LISD school board president when the case ended and praises the achievements of the desegregation plan. "I think the district has continued to follow what was laid out in the desegregation plan in offering opportunities to students throughout the district," he says. "That is where the magnet schools and other good programs originated."[42]

When Judge Woodward died in October of 2000, much of his obituary was dedicated to his guidance of the Lubbock desegregation case. Lubbock lawyer Kevin Glasheen was involved in the closing stages of the suit and says of Woodward, "I think he was one of the most respected judges who ever sat over there. Both plaintiffs and defendants thought they could get a fair trial." Of course, in between his many rulings and demands to equalize the Lubbock public-school system, Woodward negotiated a single-member system for LISD school board elections and presided over the prolonged court case that led to the single-member system that elected T. J. Patterson and Maggie Trejo to the Lubbock city council. Through sympathy, respect, and an evenhanded response to the demands of the occasion, Woodward was able to navigate a roiling sea of change in Lubbock. His strong and steady guidance gave the city a public infrastructure that could finally welcome new voices and nurture new leadership to better represent the cultural dynamics of the community.[43]

As a journalist and a Lubbock city council member, Patterson became a significant force in shaping a more diverse and equitable city during these seminal years of change. Patterson remained in his position as Texas Tech assistant dean until 1984, when he resigned to dedicate his full attention to the *Southwest Digest* and its readership, only to be drawn into the political arena that same year. Nevertheless, helping to manage the *Southwest Digest* along with his partner Eddie Richardson remained an elemental part of Patterson's daily routine. In fact, he has remained a newspaperman through all of his professional enterprises, since the opportunity first presented itself with the *Carver Heights News* in 1968. Through his newspaper articles and advertising work, Patterson has always stayed close to his neighborhood, keeping his ear to the ground to understand the needs and concerns of the Eastside and make these needs known in print. Writing, editing, and management of black weekly newspapers has been his longtime occupation, culminating in the founding and management of the *Lubbock Digest* in 1977 and a recognition of its expanded reach with the name change to the *Southwest Digest* in 1982. He understands his involvement in newspaper publishing as part of his Christian mission. “Because,” he says, “you have to stand up . . . if you believe in the good book [and what] it tells you to do . . . be your brother’s keeper, be concerned about the little folk.”

From the beginning Patterson and Richardson dedicated themselves to improving the quality of life for people living in East Lubbock, and readers of their newspaper quickly learned that the editors were fervently against drugs. The newspaper included a weekly police report column and consistently exposed the names and illegal activities of drug dealers, even publishing photographs of the traffickers. “If you got the gumption to sell drugs,” Patterson warns, “we got the gumption to show your mug shot. Oh yeah, we’d do that, man, show your pictures.”[44]

Both Patterson and Richardson were always quick to take to the streets. They participated in a myriad of local protest rallies and knocked on doors to get out the vote during election time. They also organized many antidrug marches. Patterson was always out front in these rallies, taking marchers into the neighborhoods of known drug dealers, often stopping at their houses and loudly praying for them to change their ways for their sakes and those of the children around them. He remained fearless throughout, trusting that his life was in the hands of the Almighty. One time, even when one of the marchers saw a man holding a shotgun inside the house, Patterson continued praying for the man to change his ways and concluded the march peacefully.

Patterson insists that Eastside residents Fay Brown and Reggie Andrews were the catalyst for the drug marches, and as he gained influence in his role as Lubbock city councilman, he was able to engage many civic leaders and elected officials in the activity. Of course, Bobbie Patterson and Eddie Richardson, along with many other East Lubbock residents, participated in the marches on a regular basis, and as the years went by, they were joined by people from the broader community. Lubbock Mayors Windy Sitton and David Langston marched, as well as Lubbock city council members Ty Cooke, Max Ince, and Randy Neugebauer. The clergy also joined the effort, including Reverends B. R. Moton, Larry Brooks, Wendell Davis, and J. J. Jerome Johnson. As an indication of Patterson's growing reach as a community and political leader, he succeeded in bringing US Congressman Max Thornberry from Amarillo and City Councilman Alton Hall from Plainview to Lubbock to join the protest. Over the years Patterson has conducted more than eighty neighborhood drug marches. "My brother died in California on crack," he explains. "That's why I'm against drugs. That's why I go to the street without fear or favor."

In 1989, as he was beginning his fifth year as a Lubbock city councilman, Patterson learned of another mission being developed in the nation's capital by black civil-rights activist Jesse Jackson. "I knew Jesse Jackson was visiting the jails in Washington, DC, and I liked what he was doing," he says. In 1988 Jesse Jackson ran for US president. During the primary, when he was campaigning against Michael Dukakis, he came to Lubbock for a breakfast rally at the KoKo Palace, inspiring the packed crowd with his famous speech alluding to his grandmother's patchwork quilt as a symbol of the nation. Patterson met him then and contacted him on a trip to Washington, DC, to ask him about his jail mission. "He told me he was trying to keep people out of jail. I said, 'When I get back to Lubbock, we can do something like that.'" Patterson decided that he would visit jailed prisoners during the Christmas season, including those who had been abandoned by their families. "So the next year . . . , with the help of Almighty God and my wife supporting me, we did that. We've done that about twenty-five or twenty-six years," he says in 2015.

These Christmastime visits to the county jail have made a lasting impression on Patterson, whose preacher-man style of public address rolls full volume as he tries to help those he meets on this yearly sojourn. "I look at all them in the eyes," he says, "all hip-hop gangbangers, most local. I tell them, 'The fellow making money with hip-hop won't get you none. You're a slave. That's worse slavery than my grandmother, who was owned by white folk. . . . You think about that. You commit a crime you pay the price, right? I don't support you when you do wrong because you don't have to do wrong. But at the same time, you have to understand what's happening; you have to understand what's happening, man.'"

The visits have been a mission of understanding, Patterson explains. "What I learned from these folk, a lot of them are guilty. They got to pay for what they've done, but they have no family support. They have no support at home. . . . I come to find out that when you visit these jails a lot of the relatives don't visit those folks that are locked down. . . . Sometime you're able to help someone, I've met them all the time. They appreciate

[you] being there, and some of them are doing better."

Patterson's Christmas Crusade is welcomed by most he has visited, and one former inmate went out of her way to show her appreciation to him. "I met a young lady," he remembers. "She lived here [in jail] two years, and she said, 'Mr. Patterson, I'm not going to be in next Christmas.' She was not there next year. She came by and saw me before I went to the jail. She said, 'I told you I'm not going back anymore.' My point is that many of us make mistakes. Many of us get caught. We're going to get caught, but the same time, you can reach and stand up."[45]

In a 2009 interview Eddie Richardson said of Patterson's inmate visits, "A lot of those people, you know, they are still some mother's child, and a lot of them don't get any visitors on the holidays. He goes just to make his presence there with them." He admires Patterson for his giving spirit: "Sometimes he puts Lubbock and others ahead of himself, in fact, most of the time."

While Patterson brought citywide attention to the concerns of the Eastside through his public events and work on the city council, Eddie Richardson concentrated his efforts on organizing within the black community. In 1966 he moved to Lubbock, where his mother lived, and worked for an insurance company, then took the position as director of the Opportunities Industrialization Center. "The manpower training program gave our clients the basics," Richardson explains. "Teaching minorities how to do applications, how to dress and how to speak. We taught them good grooming, hygiene, all those things. That's what made the program so different." The same year that he and Patterson founded the *Lubbock Digest*, in 1977, Richardson organized the Lubbock Black Chamber of Entrepreneurs to create a network of black business owners. He continued to focus his energies on black empowerment efforts for the next thirty years. "I want to be a tax base not a tax burden," Richardson says in the 2009 interview. "I make a lot of black folks mad with a lot of my stuff. You can't beg and bargain at the same time. You can't go out there and claim civil rights twelve months of the year and then come and ask, 'Help me with my son; help me with my family.'" While he preached a strong gospel of individual responsibility, he also recognized the engrained strictures placed on the black community and advocated loudly to rectify these injustices.

In 1989 he helped organize the Lubbock chapter of the United Black Coalition, making it one of the strongest political organizations in Lubbock. "When we first started," Richardson says, "we had a meeting, and we demanded the sheriff and the chief of police, the mayor, all the bigwigs who ran Lubbock [attend]. T. J. was also a part of the organization, and we demanded them to come to a meeting and hear what we had to say." When the meeting occurred, the chief of police got a firsthand view of the problems in East Lubbock. "Well," Richardson explains, "somebody stole a radio out of the chief's car, and we called police, and it took twenty minutes to get there. And we said, 'This is what we're saying. See how long it took and this was a fast time.' Sometimes we would call, and they wouldn't even show up."

Richardson and Patterson proceeded in their service to the community through decidedly different styles, but they were one in their commitment to black empowerment. They had both been raised in the Jim Crow South and came of age during the violent struggles of the early civil-rights movement. They were determined to change the limited opportunities of black people in Lubbock, Texas. Richardson says of Patterson, "One of the things I kid him about all the time is that he sees things in a fairyland situation. He thinks everything is perfect and right. He believes that. Over my adult years, I guess T. J. has been the closest thing I have had to a brother, but even they fuss and fight sometimes."

Richardson was born in Carrollton, Mississippi, in 1936 and grew up in Louisiana. He sees a racial contrast in his upbringing and that of Patterson's. "My mother was a rape child," he says. "The mailman got my grandmother pregnant." He goes on to note that it went unreported because it was not unusual for white men to take their pleasure with black girls in Mississippi back then. "The difference between there and out here is there was a lot of segregation and not a lot of integration." He proceeds to illustrate this conundrum: "I had an uncle who died and a group of us were headed down to the funeral and a state trooper stopped us and then we got to talking and told him we were down there for a funeral and so and so and, through talking to the state trooper, found out they were kin." Richardson reiterates, "A white state trooper stopped the black folks and discovered they were kin. You had more interracial stuff in the Deep South than you did any place else."

Richardson uses himself as an example of that "interracial stuff" by pointing out that he has "all different kinds of white in me. When I was a baby, my daddy was light and my mother was real light. My mother, when I was a baby, she said one white woman told another white woman, 'You know that little nigger gal had a white baby. Did you see the momma? Have you seen the daddy?'" He ascribes his confrontational style to his light color. "Because of my color, I always tried to prove I was black," he says. "That's why I was a so-called militant."[46]

Richardson achieved his worldly ways and acerbic style in the military. Before he graduated from high school, he enlisted in the United States Air Force, where he served with the Strategic Air Command for ten years. He spent seven of those years playing saxophone with the *Tops in Blue*, the Air Force international variety show that entertained military, civilian, and school groups. He reached the regional, national, and international levels of annual competition three times during those performing years and was named "Airman of the Month" numerous times. Richardson earned his GED, then attended college at each of his duty stations, earning approximately three hundred total credit hours in various classes that ranged from cooking to railway maintenance to Russian history when he was stationed in Alaska. He received the Outstanding Educational Achievement Award before earning a degree in human relations from McNeese State College in Lake Charles, Louisiana.[47]

As with most minorities who served in the military in World War II, Korea, and the early years of the Vietnam War, racial discrimination back home became a stunning affront. In his 2009 interview Richardson enjoys telling a particularly gratifying discrimination story from his service days in the 1950s. "For some reason, I had everybody's meal ticket," he says. "We were on the train, and we went into some restaurant, and they wouldn't let us in, and they told me we had to eat in the kitchen. And I told them I wasn't going in the kitchen. I said, 'I tell you what, I've got the ticket, and I'm not going to sign it if I can't eat,' and what they did was they fixed the plates for all of us." That kind of pushback from Eddie Richardson became his signature style through all his years in Lubbock. "You see, I used to be called the town militant," he says with pride.

There is no doubt that Richardson has always had a more jaded view of the human spirit than Patterson. "A lot of social things T. J. and I don't agree on because I don't believe everything people tell me like T. J. does. Prove it to me," Richardson insists. "People made me that way because people used me. I've been used a lot." That chip on his shoulder has translated into many years of powerful and effective editorial columns calling the question on the local, white power structure and black apathy. His professional efforts are dedicated to changing both.

To encourage a sense of black pride in the American experience, Richardson worked directly with Houston state representative Al Edwards in his lobbying efforts to make Texas the first state to recognize Juneteenth as a state holiday. Edward's bill was enacted in 1980, with Juneteenth established as a partial staffing holiday. Today, most states observe June 19 through special Juneteenth celebrations of that significant day in 1865 when Texas announced the abolition of slavery. Juneteenth has been expanded nationwide to become a celebration of emancipation of the slaves throughout the Confederate South and was recognized by the US Congress as Juneteenth Independence Day in 1996. Richardson served as the director of the Lubbock Juneteenth Commission for many years, coordinating and building the local celebration into a widely attended public event. In 1997 Richardson was appointed by Governor George W. Bush to serve on the newly established Texas Juneteenth Cultural and Historical Commission to coordinate local and state celebrations of this growing acknowledgment of Freedom Day.[48]

Richardson also served on the board of Habitat for Humanity, as secretary of the board of directors for the South Plains Community Action Association, and on the board of Assault on Illiteracy program. He has always been a vocal and committed champion of early-childhood education, and through his all-out efforts in support of the Head Start program, the Eddie Richardson Head Start Preschool and Daycare at 1110 Fortieth Street has been named in his honor.

The public response that Eddie Richardson and T. J. Patterson have received through their community activism is a significant sign of the cultural changes that have taken place in Lubbock since the 1960s. By the mid-1970s, ethnic identity was something to proclaim rather than hide, and in addition to the *Lubbock Digest*, Bidal Aguero founded *El Editor* in 1977 as a Hispanic weekly newspaper that focused on the concerns of a growing Lubbock Latino community. Both these publications were established with an activist mission.

The publications of Patterson, Richardson, Aguero, and his wife, Olga Aguero, have sought to influence elections by endorsing candidates, mobilizing voters, and addressing the issues that directly affect the black and Hispanic communities in Lubbock and nationwide. Much copy has been dedicated to respective cultural heroes. Cesar Chavez and the achievements of the United Farm Workers Union; LISD board member Linda DeLeon, in her battle to save Thompson Junior High during the Lubbock desegregation case; and San Antonio Mayor Henry Cisneros, have all been featured in *El Editor*. Reverend Martin Luther King, Reverend Jesse Jackson, Texas Representative Al Edwards, US Supreme Court Justice Thurgood Marshall, and US President Barack Obama have all taken their places stage center in the pages of the *Southwest Digest*. For almost forty years both these publications have remained meaningful voices for their ethnic communities, urging their readers to get involved in public life through challenging, sometimes downright stinging, editorials leveled against white privilege and minority complacency.

Articles in *El Editor* are sometimes written in Spanish and English. In 1967 Ernesto Barton established the first all-Spanish radio station and explained the challenge and significance to *Avalanche-Journal* reporter Doug Hensley: "When we applied for the first all-Spanish radio station in Lubbock, people thought we were out of our mind. We got our station on the air, and the tornado hit. We were broadcasting side by side with KFYO, which was the emergency station at the time. We were broadcasting in Spanish and provided interpreters for some of the agencies helping tornado victims." Hensley notes, "The work was so exemplary that Barton later received a commendation from President Nixon recognizing the station for service to the community." From 1972 until 2013, Barton also produced a weekly Spanish and English television program called *Si Se Puede*, a title alluding to the rallying cry of cultural icon Cesar Chavez in his successful fight for higher farm-worker wages during the 1960s and 1970s. In 2008 Barack Obama appropriated the term in both English and Spanish. "Yes We Can" and "Si Se Puede" became the rallying cry for his successful presidential campaign. By 1979 Barton had established a second community newspaper, the *West Texas Hispanic Times*.[49]

All of these minority media outlets have consistently served as a counterpoint to the *Avalanche-Journal*, the daily newspaper that has been a part of Lubbock history under one form of its present name or another since May 4, 1900. It remains a very successful enterprise and has played a significant role in representing the opinions of the majority community, including leading efforts to keep black citizens residentially isolated in the 1920s and efforts to keep the Lubbock city council at-large election system in the 1980s. "I've seen ten or twelve general media papers fail because none of them could survive with the *A-J*," says Eddie Richardson, who consistently calls the *Avalanche-Journal* by its nickname, the *A-J*. "We survived because we didn't try to compete." The *Southwest Digest* was designed to serve the special interests of the black community as a weekly, and Richardson and Patterson had no interest in the folly of expanding its focus, although they were certainly interested in expanding its readership.

In a moment of sheer bravado, Richardson and Patterson approached the *Avalanche-Journal* marketing director, Norval Pollard, with a possible partnership, a testament in itself to the expanding cultural sensibilities of this longstanding rock-rib, conservative, white newspaper. Pollard was responsive to their appeal, and the *Southwest Digest* began to be inserted into many copies of the *Avalanche-Journal* each Friday, the day after publication of the weekly. Richardson explains, "T. J. and I and Norval went out and knocked on doors and from there started building relationships. One of the things we figured out is there are places we can go that the *A-J* can't go . . . and places the *A-J* can go that we can't go. We're the most read newspaper in East Lubbock on publication day. We've got more subscribers over here than the *A-J*." Richardson recalls how the tentative agreement was sealed one day when he and Patterson were visiting Pollard. "We just happened to be there and a lady calls," says Richardson, "a white woman, and she was mad there was no *Southwest Digest* in her *A-J* paper that day. We had a big laugh about it."[50]

That a copy of the *Southwest Digest* could arrive at houses tucked into the Friday edition of the *Avalanche-Journal* is a true signal of a growing cultural fluidity in the city of Lubbock. While the struggle for ethnic equality began with strong federal pressure to integrate Texas Tech and the public schools, it came to fruition through the implementation of single-member districts in local elections. As the first African American to serve on the Lubbock City Council, T. J. Patterson greeted the challenges of representing the newly constituted District 2 with enthusiasm and anticipation from his first day on the job.

Chapter 5
City Days and City Ways

Even with five candidates running in the very first District 2 Lubbock city council election, T. J. Patterson won the position without a runoff. He received over twice as many votes as the next in number, and the success of his race is a testament to his campaigning abilities and his longtime involvement in the Eastside community. Among those who savored his victory were Patterson's neighbors, Edwin Scott and his wife, Pearlene. Scott arrived in Lubbock in 1944 from Rockdale, Texas, and was working at Reeds Grocery on Nineteenth Street when he first met Patterson in 1959. He credits the election win to Patterson's speaking ability. "He's a good speaker," Scott says, "and every time [T. J. was asked to speak, he went]. Bet'cha there never was a week that he stayed home." Patterson says that, at the time, he didn't care if he won or not, but when he was elected, he considered it not so much a personal victory as "a victory for all of us."[1]

Alan Henry, Lubbock mayor in 1984, remembers his anxiety about this new configuration of city counsel representatives. Henry had served on the Lubbock city council since 1976 and was confident that he had the experience and temperament to meet the challenge of this new arrangement of political parts, but no one really knew what to expect. "During those times, members of the council more or less earned their stripes in the community before running for city council, working with United Way or various projects that got would-be council members to be known in the community," he explains. In this first single-member election, two council members were well-known incumbents. Joan Baker and E. Jack Brown both chose to run in their newly designated districts. Four others were new to this particular political arena. Bob Nash, a well-known local broadcaster, ran in the new District 4; George Carpenter stepped up to represent central Lubbock in District 3. Maggie Trejo joined the council representing District 1, and T. J. Patterson represented District 2.

Mayor Henry was aware of the checkered history of other Texas cities that had gone to single-member districts, with results ranging from "complete unity to complete chaos, depending on the city and the makeup of the council." Naturally, he greeted the first single-member city council meetings with some apprehension and was relieved to find that the change went very smoothly, thanks, in large part, to the personalities and perceptions of the two minority representatives. Henry credits the easy transition to the fact that Patterson and Trejo were already known to the wider community and both had public knowledge and support. They quickly proved that, while they represented the voters of their districts, they understood their responsibilities to all of Lubbock. Henry also credits the sensibilities of the rest of the council for the constructive spirit of that first single-member city council. All members recognized their responsibilities as they sailed into the unchartered waters that lay ahead. "Whatever Maggie or T. J. did," Henry says, "it was going to be groundbreaking as far as representing their districts, and the same thing for the other members of the council."

While all council members have continued to take district issues very seriously, there has also remained a commitment to citywide decision making, a balance established in the first single-member council. "Lubbock's city council has in one way an at-large mentality, as far as city projects," Henry says. "That sort of thing has been maintained, and I think for the better." He recalls asking the mayor of a major Texas city just what issues were determined by single-member districts. The mayor replied, "Virtually everything, including where to place . . . stoplights. If it was one person's district, they made the decision, not the council at large." Henry is pleased that Lubbock has not followed that example, pointing out that "there are so many issues that have nothing to do with the neighborhoods."[2]

When Patterson stepped into his new role, he embraced his responsibilities with a humble receptivity. He always remembered that his pastor at the Bethel AME Church, Reverend A. W. Wilson, had run for the Lubbock city council in 1964 and lost under the at-large system. Patterson felt a special kinship with the pastor as he assumed his new position. He also recognized the importance of learning how to effect change through the internal workings of city government and his public duties. "One of the first assignments I received," Patterson remembers, "was to go to a ribbon cutting at Diana's Dollhouse in Memphis Place Mall." The occasion couldn't help but bring back memories of the many times and places that black citizens of Lubbock weren't welcome on the west side of town. "When we walked in there," he says, "I had just been elected, and they all looked at me funny, but I was so excited, and I noticed they had white carpet. And Satan got in my head. I went and got a cup of coffee and wanted to spill it on the rug, but I didn't want to sink down that low."[3]

Besides attending official public events, Patterson learned quickly that much of the work of the council proceeded through responses to a vast number of boards and commissions made up of city staff and citizen volunteers appointed by council members. The council periodically heard from boards that managed the Memorial Civic Center, the airport, the city library system, the city bus system, the ever-complicated municipal utilities, public health, animal rescue, and many others. Of course, the council also responded to the direct needs of city departments, including the police department, the fire department, parks and recreation, planning and zoning, plus building permits, streets, water, and all the other management structures necessary to run a city of 186,000 people in 1984.

Knowing who could actually make a decision and approve a project, rather than who might have just enough power to hinder or frustrate an issue, was of great value, and Patterson determined to learn how to steer a cause or project past the right board or official and deal with the inevitable quagmire of procedures, rules, and contacts confronting him on the way. "Texas is a home-rule state, and cities lack the authority and autonomy that most citizens think they have," Patterson explains. "State legislation must pass on both the house and senate sides. Cities can't arbitrarily do something that is out of step with the state house." He expands on the point. "The governing rules and procedures are far more complicated than most voters understand. I've seen my folks talking about taxes, going on about the Taxation Equalization Board. Hell, that's in the governor's office. You can't get nothing done about that."

Of course, the layers of bureaucracy that often bedevil communications between groups frustrated Patterson. He remembers a case when the city of Lubbock was dealing with Texas Tech University. Relying on his experience in the business college, he told the other council members that when they had major projects with Texas Tech, it made sense to deal with the board of regents and not the president or chancellor. "Hell, they're hired folk. Go to those who set policy. That's how you do that." He recounts a typical failure to communicate with the top decision makers. "We lost a fire station out there on the campus because we were dealing with the staff." He points out, "We should have been dealing with the board of regents, appointed by the governor, sanctioned by the senate, right?"[4]

Patterson had spent his whole adult life as a grassroots activist and understood instantly how important it was to work in solid partnership with Maggie Trejo, the new council member from District 1, representing the predominantly Hispanic neighborhoods of the city. Over the years Patterson had taken every opportunity to join African American and Hispanic forces to effect policy, but with few exceptions the traditional geographic divide of the minority population limited his efforts. He names Jose Ramirez as one of the exceptions. Ramirez was a Borden's milkman with a delivery route in East Lubbock before he established Jose's Restaurant at Fiftieth Street and Avenue H. Ramirez was one of the first Hispanics in Lubbock to be active in the Republican Party. In 1984 he was elected to the Lubbock Independent School District board of trustees, and in 1987 LISD named the new magnet school at 702 Avenue T the Jose Ramirez Elementary School in his honor.

Patterson also celebrates the outreach efforts of Jorge Moreno, who became a very successful Hispanic leader through his business, La Feria, originally a dry-goods store catering to visiting Mexican farm workers or braceros. He named the store after his hometown, La Feria, just west of Harlingen in South Texas. Moreno later expanded the business to include Tejano records, tapes, and CDs and developed this offering into a very broad-based niche market in Tejano music, early and late. Moreno was a champion of Hispanic and citywide causes, especially for Lubbock youth, and Patterson admired his efforts.[5] However, it was through his partnership with Maggie Trejo on the Lubbock city council that Patterson finally found the means to represent the needs of the whole minority community and effect significant change.

Like Patterson, Trejo won her election without a runoff, campaigning against four other candidates for the first District 1 seat on the council. Trejo explains how she decided to stand for the office. "We had this young lady who had moved to our district, and it didn't sit very well. Here we had been fighting [for] single-member districts forever and ever. She then decides to move into our area and represent our district? I don't think so! That's why I ran."

Trejo had worked as the administrative assistant for Texas District 83 Representative Froy Salinas and understood the importance of finding an effective voice for the community. "I like helping people. . . . I had worked with Froy Salinas. I loved that kind of work, but never in my life did I think that I would be running for office," she exclaims. "I understood that we needed representation from our district because, really, if you look back at the history of Lubbock . . . administrative positions were just not there." Trejo won the election without the support of the Hispanic newspaper, *El Editor*, and savors her victory. "It was exciting. I had never been the public person or things like that. It was exciting to see your friends there, your supporters. It was just an exciting time . . . because they were working so hard, and I think that's what I remember most. People really cared, kind of like Obama now. People were so excited they were going to get a representative from the district." It was from her broad perspective on politics and her roots in the Lubbock Hispanic community that Trejo found the inspiration to run for office and serve on the council in partnership with T. J. Patterson.[6]

Born Magdalena de la Rosa in 1942, Maggie Trejo moved with her family to Lubbock when she was three years old. She grew up during the time when many Hispanics were beginning to settle down in Lubbock rather than just pass through. By the 1950s Lubbock cotton farming was becoming more and more mechanized. Seasonal farm labor was less in demand. Hispanics who had come each year to work the fall cotton harvest began to settle in and build a community. In 1950 there were 11,642 Hispanics living in Lubbock County. In 1960 there were 17,003. In 1970 there were 31,082, and in 1980 there were 41,428, representing 20 percent of the population.[7] A reminiscence by Rufus Martinez, who first came to town in 1959, describes a familiar pattern. "When I first came to Lubbock," he says, "it was in the summer to chop cotton and earn money for my school clothes. Then I would go back to Calvert, my hometown. I came after my last year of college at Sam Houston State, and didn't go back. I married my wife, and I've been here ever since." In 1963 Martinez bought a Mobil service station at Twenty-fifth and Avenue H and became partners with Glynn Morgan. He muses on the engrained cultural attitudes of his customers. "I remember when I first started out, people would come to the station and wonder where the boss was. I would tell them I was the boss. Then they'd ask where the manager was. I said I was the manager. They'd ask where the owner was, and I said I was the owner."[8]

Trejo and Martinez are about the same age and represent that first generation of Hispanics who were solidly rooted in the Lubbock Hispanic community, a close-knit group defined by a city color line that included designated seating in movie theaters, designated shopping areas, and any other business with a sign posted, "We Reserve the Right to Refuse Service to Anyone." However, growing up, Trejo didn't experience these forms of discrimination. "I was raised here in Lubbock," she says, "but I really think my dad was very smart because he never took us to places where they said 'No! You cannot come here.' I never went through that. . . . If we went to the movies, we went to the Mexican movies, and we had a ball and what have you. But we never went to places where we were not wanted."

When Trejo was finally confronted with the rigid cultural lines of demarcation engrained in the town, it didn't hurt her feelings. It made her mad. "You know when I found out about discrimination?" She asks. "I was already going with my husband, going to Slaton, and we went to this little drugstore, and we're sitting there to get some Cokes. . . . I remember this man pointed to the wall, and I didn't even think of anything, but my friend Rosie said, 'Let's go.' I was so dumb, and then when she told me that didn't hurt me. I was angry. That's better than being humiliated. So I was very fortunate. My dad, he knew better, so he didn't take us to places where we weren't wanted." Richard Lopez served for more than thirty years as executive director of the Guadalupe Economic Services Corporation. He was also the cofounder of the very successful and dynamic South Plains Food Bank. Trejo quotes him as saying, "It won't change until everybody who feels that way dies."[9]

Trejo attended Lubbock High School and graduated in 1961. Alan Henry was one of her classmates. "Alan and I went to school together," she points out, "and I really believe when you come from a school that says 'sportsmanship then victory,' it stays in you. Lubbock High had that." Throughout her schooling from Sanders Elementary to Thompson Junior High to Lubbock High School, Trejo took her studies seriously and credits her achievements to her father's protection and her teachers' support. "I didn't have a problem in school," she says. "My last name is de la Rosa and there were two de la Rosa kids that were ahead of me, and they were smart. So they assumed I was their little sister, so the teachers treated me fine. I never had a problem with any of my teachers. In fact, when I ran for office, who were my helpers? Some of my teachers."

Her junior year she married Louis Trejo, then went through a bout of rheumatic fever and developed rheumatoid arthritis. "So," she says, "for about ten years everybody kept telling me I was going to be crippled, and one day, I said 'No, I'm not!' I got sick and tired of it. So, here I am, still walking around and everything." After some eighteen years of raising her son and battling her illness, Trejo determined to pursue a degree at Texas

Tech University, and as it turned out, T. J. Patterson was her advisor. "I went to talk to T. J. because I was thinking maybe I shouldn't take a class, and T. J. said, 'You can do it. You can do it!'" Trejo received her degree in business management from Texas Tech in 1979 and, among many other enterprises, built her own real-estate company.

When Trejo and Patterson took their places on the dais as the first Hispanic and first African American council members, the Lubbock city council was stepping into a new city hall and a new era of municipal needs and challenges. Trejo explains, "The city was seventy-five years old when we got there, so we did a lot of new things, like major projects, including solid waste issues, the airport remodeling, and even the generator for Texas Tech. There were just a lot of things we did. We were so busy, we didn't have the time to bicker with each other. We were just so busy." The alliance between Trejo and Patterson was an elemental dynamic in the decision making of the new council. "It was wonderful working with T. J.," Trejo says. "He and I were one, and we stuck together, and that surprised the heck out of the other council people. They learned very quickly if they wanted us to be positive about their things, they need to also listen to what we have to say. . . . I told them, 'You better stick together because T. J. and I have leverage' because they knew all you needed sometimes was four votes, so there were two—Maggie and T. J."

This Patterson-Trejo leverage was often the deciding factor in council votes. Trejo says, "I would get there at 7:30 a.m. and say, 'All right, whoever wants to talk to me?' And they would come if they had something they wanted me to help them with. . . . You see, we didn't do our fighting in the public. . . . We did it behind closed doors." Trejo says she and Patterson did not really experience any overt discrimination at City Hall, but she does think some council members thought they were "kind of naïve." She recalls an attempt by E. Jack Brown to allow a trailer camp on Quaker and Erskine in Trejo's district. She had done her homework and was opposed to it. "I foresaw the city was growing that way," she explains. "So, we were ready for them, and they needed a six-one vote. He didn't get it, and he was shocked."

During a trip to Washington, DC, when the council members were on a break, Trejo says, "He came over and said, "Maggie and T. J., can I talk to you a minute?' We said, 'Okay,' and then he said, 'You know, the way we do business in the city is we don't talk about things until we're in the meeting.' And so he was, in a kind of bad way, telling us we had gotten together on this vote, and it really shocked me. . . . I didn't say much, but then when we sat down again together, I said, 'I didn't really understand what you were saying, but I worked for a state representative, and what do you think they do when they are walking around getting votes for their projects?' So, he didn't say much. . . . He brought it back again, that same project, and he was sitting next to me that time and goes 'Maggie, how do you feel about that project?' And I said, 'It's not going to go.'"

Even with their disagreements on policy, Trejo praises that first single-member city council for always trying to work as a united force and mentions that the Standard and Poor's bond rating committee was surprised to be able to go over the bond rates with all city council members in attendance at one meeting, rather than have to hold three or four meetings to inform individual council members. This first single-member council took its responsibilities very seriously, and Trejo notes a visit from then–San Antonio Mayor Henry Cisneros as another example. "We were all sitting together as a council, and he looked at us and said, 'A council that sits together and eats together will do great things.' I never knew any different," she says, and elaborates on the public outreach of this council. "I had never worked with blacks. . . . We were kind of segregated ourselves, you know; we were all Hispanics. . . . I never had been close to blacks. . . . When I really got to know the black community was when I became a councilwoman. I would go to their functions, and I got to meet a lot of people." She goes on to explain, "I think people were curious, and I gained twenty pounds . . . because people were always inviting us places. I was going everywhere. . . . Alan took his kids and wife to all the activities—going, going, going. You see, he brought his kids up right. He took them to all activities. It didn't matter if it was the black community, the Hispanic community. The kids learned to appreciate all of that."[10]

Besides his inclusive social calendar, Mayor Alan Henry's administrative goals were also inclusive. He points out the significance of that unified council during the prolonged permitting process for a new city water source at Justiceburg, Texas. Henry believes this project was the most important responsibility of his mayoral tenure and certainly the prime example of an issue that required an at-large approach to governance. Securing permits, making applications, holding hearings, and addressing two federal lawsuits by landowners remained an ongoing challenge for the council throughout Henry's two terms as mayor. In 1986, shortly before he left office, the lawsuits were finally dropped and the engineering studies completed for the location of the dam. Henry says, "The city council that was in office after I retired, under the leadership of Mayor Peck McMinn, was very generous in the naming of the project in my honor." Lake Alan Henry was destined to become a new recreational and residential site for the people of the area and a secure water source for the city of Lubbock in the near future.[11]

Henry is also quick to point out how important the two minority members were in bringing the council a better understanding of city issues affecting their districts. A significant example of this new understanding occurred when Interstate 27 was extended from its original North Loop 289 point to Eighty-second Street in south Lubbock. The change threatened to physically separate the predominately minority portion of Lubbock from the rest of the city. Alan mentions how Patterson often felt a personal ownership of certain concerns. "Every once in a while, we would have some issue that was coming up, and you knew T. J. had certain issues that were his issues. When other members of the council would start talking about what T. J. felt like was his issue, he would say, 'Wait a minute, you're hoeing on my row.'" The change to Interstate 27 was a problem that Patterson most definitely considered a row that was his to hoe, and he did. Henry explains, "The chamber of commerce and everybody got on board for that interstate highway. Well, there were some people like me and T. J. and Eddie Richardson that said, 'Wait a minute, what you're doing is just building a barrier between the city and us.' He could recognize the difference between an issue that sounded good as far as for consumption in his district and an issue that really had a chance of going somewhere. . . . Now, that's the kind of rows he hoed."

The solution to the Interstate 27 problem was to use city funds and build an overpass that extends Martin Luther King, Jr. Boulevard south over the railroad tracks, allowing the southern parts of the city to connect from east to west. To Henry, the solution to this problem shows how representation from all parts of the city can illuminate an issue and lead to a meaningful resolution.

The more time that Henry spent with Patterson, the more he grew to respect him, especially when they were off the dais and out of the glare of the television lights. "I have never met anyone so sincere and [who] felt more strongly about his responsibilities," Henry says, "because here is someone who had campaigned all his life for some of the issues in East Lubbock, and now he was in the position to do something about it."[12]

One of the first things Patterson decided to act on for the people of East Lubbock was to make the federal holiday of Dr. Martin Luther King, Jr.'s birthday into a four-day Lubbock celebration. Originally coordinated by

Joan Ervin and later by the Martin Luther King Commemorative Council, the birthday celebration is always open to the public and includes an awards banquet, a youth night, a citywide worship service, and a night of gospel music. The four-day event is a tribute to the inspiration and leadership that Dr. Martin Luther King brought to the struggle for civil rights and a joyous acknowledgment of the contributions that the Lubbock black community has to offer the whole city.[13]

In 1993 Patterson was officiating at the Martin Luther King celebration and looked out to see his biological father sitting in the audience. He recalls the event. "'Ladies and gentlemen,' I said, 'I want you to meet my father, Mr. Samuel Collins, who is sitting here tonight.' Then I said, 'Stand up, Daddy, so these citizens of Lubbock can meet you! He stood up, and I felt real good. I was just thinking, here I have my father in the audience, and I didn't know much about him, and here he was! What a blessing. I don't want to take anything away from what Hershiel had done. This was just something which was very hard to do."

Patterson's public reunion with his biological father had been a very long time in coming. Hershiel Patterson adopted him and raised him, and his mother never talked about Samuel Collins, but Patterson began to get glimmers of his story when he was a teenager. He learned his birth name when he was fifteen. "I was shooting pool one day," Patterson remembers. "I snuck in the back of a pool hall in Wichita Falls. In those days, if you weren't eighteen, you couldn't go into the joint. But if you behaved yourself, the pool hall man would let you stay. At the pool hall the houseman said, 'I know your daddy.' I said, 'Yeah, my daddy is Hershiel Patterson.' And he said, 'No, that's not your daddy. Your daddy is Sam, Sam Collins. That's your daddy, Sam Collins.'"

Patterson continues with his origin story. "And, of course, that bothered me because my mother never told me about that. So I went home, and she didn't want to talk about it. See, I am named after his uncle, Thomas James Collins. . . . Yeah, my mother and father, they didn't stay married long. They broke up about the time I was born. My mother was in the eleventh grade. . . . In those days, high school was only eleven grades for blacks. She finished school, then I was born."

Ever the good son who became a good father, Patterson quickly interjects one of his frequent admonitions. "Black kids today don't understand concern of family. All we've got is family, especially don't mistreat mama." In his teen years, the rule of not mistreating mama extended to not asking questions that mama did not want to discuss. Patterson was thirty-two years old and back from Vietnam before he began to feel compelled to find his biological father, and it turned out to be as easy as finding the right relative. "I can remember one day when Aunt April Rose Hobdy attempted to tell me, but I paid no attention," he says. "Once the word gets out, he's not hard to find. . . . Plus, my cousin's mother was in Wichita Falls as well, so we called her. . . . I went and found him. You can't not know about him. My mother wouldn't tell me."

Patterson learned that Samuel Collins had played a little football for Huston Tillotson College, then ended up in San Antonio, where he was a bartender at Kelly Air Force Base for more than forty years. That's where they first met. "I stopped him, and I wanted to go drink whiskey with him. I wanted to prove to my dad that I was a man. I figured the only way to prove that was to drink liquor with him," Patterson sighs. "But I got drunk. Before I got drunk, we went to go see Miss Wiggles out there at the club. She'd wiggle her head and her chest. He wanted me to see all of that. I wanted to be big and strong, you know. I was just trying. I was trying so hard to prove that I am a man." Following this meeting Patterson sought out his brothers and sisters on the Collins side of the family. There are five: Juanita, Carolyn, Evelyn, Cecilia, and Sam, Jr. He discovered that his uncle and namesake, Thomas James Collins, was a meat cutter in Cleveland, Ohio, and stood 6'5", but Patterson never met him.

After the formal introduction of his father and the end of the evening ceremonies for the Martin Luther King, Jr., celebration, Patterson drove Collins to his mother's home. Hannah came to the door, looked at Sam Collins but showed no interest or emotion. Neither his mother nor Collins made any attempt to draw closer to the other. Patterson still considers it one of the deepest regrets that he did not make the one small move necessary to bring his mother and father together to at least talk to each other after all those years of total separation. Still, it was very gratifying to see his father in that audience at the Lubbock Martin Luther King celebration while he officiated at an event that he had instituted in his role as a Lubbock city council member. He knew he had arrived as a man, in his father's eyes.[14]

As part of his responsibilities on the Lubbock city council, Patterson became the Lubbock representative to the Texas Municipal League and is a strong supporter of the mission of the organization. Founded as the League of Texas Municipalities in the summer of 1913, the purpose of the organization is to provide services to Texas cities and city officials that include legal information and advice, plus legislative representation on the state and federal levels. A member of the National League of Cities, the Texas Municipal League has over a thousand member cities, representing

98 percent of the urban population of the state.[15] "In my opinion," Patterson says, "you need it. . . . You cannot work by yourself. You have to work collectively together with people to make things happen." In that spirit of cooperation, Patterson quickly worked his way up the leadership ladder of the League. The Texas Municipal League has fifteen substate regions, which promote the interests of city government in each region. In 1989 he became secretary of Region Three, which comprises the twenty-six counties of West Texas. In 1990 he became vice president of Region Three and in 1991 president of Region Three.

In 1986 Patterson also organized the Texas Association of Black City Council Members at a time when there were only 232 black elected municipal officials in the state. Patterson remembers that "he and a few other council members were at a League meeting in 1984 when they were discussing how few opportunities there were for African Americans to be on the board of directors. The mayor of San Antonio at the time, Henry Cisneros, said he had a possible solution to their concern, and they were offered a room to host their own meeting in 1986 when the Texas Municipal League held its annual meeting." Some fifty people came to the gathering, and they organized as the Texas Association of Black City Council Members. In 2016 there were more than 400 elected black officials in Texas, and the group continued to show its deep appreciation for Patterson by hosting the annual T. J. Patterson, Sr., Annual Golf Classic. Each year a different country club is selected for the tournament from around the state and proceeds from the event go to the association's scholarship program.

Through Patterson's leadership the Texas Association of Black City Council Members approached a group of Hispanic city officials at a meeting in Corpus Christi, Texas, and helped them organize the Association of Hispanic Municipal Officials. The two organizations began working together in 1993. In 1995 Patterson ran for president of the Texas Municipal League and soon realized that some white representatives didn't want him elected. He remembers, "They tried to knock me out, but we hung in there, and we won." The joy of that moment was a sweet victory. "And we won. And we won," he repeats. "Not only that, we legally kept the Texas Association of Black City Council Members and the Association of Hispanic Municipal Officials as an auxiliary to the Texas Municipal League." That accomplishment is one that Patterson still remembers with great pride. He also remembers praying "Jesus Christ, what do I do now? I'm all over Texas from Mercedes, Brownfield, Marshall, El Paso, all over Texas seeing folk, talking to folk."

If he thought his plate was full then, he was about to add even more to the load. His next challenge would take him out of his home state and onto the national stage. Patterson became involved in the National League of Cities when Henry Cisneros was mayor of San Antonio and president of the organization. Kathryn Whitmire, mayor of Houston, was also involved in the National League and was the first female elected to city government in Houston. She served as the president of the US Conference of Mayors and the Texas Municipal League and was the first mayor of Houston to appoint an African American, Lee P. Brown, as Houston police chief. Brown would later become mayor of Houston. Whitmore extended her minority commitment to the Houston Hispanic community with the appointment of Sylvia R. Garcia as presiding judge of the Houston Municipal Court.

Cisneros and Whitmire supported Patterson's participation in the National League of Cities. He says he had "brought something to the table, and when you do that people will help you. You take advantage of the resource around you. You can't do it by yourself." Patterson was first appointed to both the Communication Policy Committee and the Transportation Policy Committee by Detroit Mayor Dennis Archer, when he was the president of the National League of Cities. He was then appointed to the Energy, Environment and Natural Resources Steering Committee and eventually served as chair, as well as serving as a member of the League board of directors. His years of active leadership in the Texas Municipal League and the National League of Cities greatly expanded his professional network and his understanding of strategies for making municipal government work.[16]

In 1993, while serving as mayor pro tem, Maggie Trejo resigned her position on the Lubbock city council to manage the Lubbock office of US Congressman Bill Sarpalius who was running for reelection in the Texas Thirteenth Congressional District. Before she left office, Trejo and Patterson took one last official trip together, and Trejo remembers it fondly. "When I was appointed by [Texas Speaker of the House] Gib Lewis to go around the state and find out why minorities weren't utilized, . . . I got to meet Regina Montoya from Dallas. When Clinton became president, she [First Lady, Hillary Clinton] invited us to a private tour at the White House. So I said, 'T. J., you are coming with me.' We were supposed to go in-and-out, but not really. We were there two hours. . . . T. J. was excited because the Black Caucus was in a meeting with Clinton, and he was beyond himself."[17]

Sarpalius was defeated in 1994, caught in what became known as the "Republican Revolution," an election that ousted numerous Democratic Party incumbents. Trejo returned to her longtime business, Maggie Trejo

Real Estate, and began working part-time with the Community Housing Resource Board. In 1996, she became executive director and in 1999 was named the Minority Small Business Advocate by the US Small Business Administration for her work with the housing board. She has continued her commitment to public service with volunteer work at the well-baby clinic and her church, Our Lady of Grace, as well as serving on numerous city commissions. In 1997 the city of Lubbock honored her by renaming the community center located in the Arnett-Benson neighborhood the Maggie Trejo Supercenter. Over the years she has been recognized by many organizations for her service to Lubbock, including being named as Woman of the Year by the League of United Latin American Citizens (LULAC) and receiving the Headliner Award, the Gold Medal Award, and the Hispania of the Year Award by Women in Communications, the George Woods Outstanding Service in Politics Award from the NAACP, and the Local Hero Award from the Lubbock Convention and Visitors Bureau.

City leaders who served with Trejo on the city council are quick to acknowledge her effective leadership. During her tenure, Mayor Henry praised her with these words, "Maggie does her homework, and she insists on having her questions answered. Yet, she is low-key and does not draw attention to herself." Trejo adds her own version of her place on the council: "They knew I had to be tough, and I wasn't really tough. . . . Sometimes you know what they would call me? The Shark. But, anyways, I had a lot of fun when I was there."[18] Just as Patterson proved to be the right man at the right time for Lubbock, so too was this strong woman that he called "sister" while others called her "Shark." Trejo was followed on the council by Victor Hernandez, who was elected to represent District 1 and who brought a more confrontational style to deliberations during his decade of service. Patterson remained a strong and steady force on the council, campaigning and winning reelection over and over again. He served for twenty years and holds the record for the longest-serving council member in Lubbock history. During his extensive and successful tenure, he served with five different mayors and eighteen different fellow council members, always approaching the dynamics of the council by building coalitions.

"You only need four," he always says about that governing body of six, and his career is a study in the art of the possible.

The city that Patterson helped guide for twenty years was a small metropolis on the move, steadily renewing its long history of economic growth after a decade on idle. The fallout from the Lubbock tornado and a weak national economy had taken its toll, but by the mid-1980s the Lubbock city council was consistently scrambling to keep up with the infrastructure needs of new development proceeding like a juggernaut south and west of the highway loop that had encircled the town since its completion in 1970. Upscale businesses were popping up all along Eighty-second Street, a thoroughfare south of Loop 289 that soon extended west beyond Slide Road, heading toward Frankford, which had been a dirt road until 1984. With residential development also quickly spreading beyond Eighty-second Street and Slide Road, Patterson joined the rest of the council in frantically trying to keep up with this mass residential movement by paving Ninety-eighth Street. Perhaps they were a bit too frantic in their efforts. The original Ninety-eighth Street roadbed was faulty, and the city returned to fix the problem, at great cost and effort, two different times before the thoroughfare successfully satisfied the traffic needs of this burgeoning new area of town.[19]

In 1995, thanks to the perseverance of then–Lubbock state senator John T. Montford, the council began its ongoing supervisory role in the building of an east-west highway through Lubbock that would efficiently connect these new areas of town with the heart of the city and confirm the engrained expectation that a person should be able to get anywhere in Lubbock in fifteen minutes. The residential and commercial growth to the south and west had broken that steadfast rule. The new highway promised to fix it. Patterson is very proud to have voted for the Lubbock city council ordinance naming the new highway the Marsha Sharp Freeway, in recognition of the very talented and popular coach of the Texas Tech University Lady Raiders, who led her 1993 team to the NCAA national basketball championship, the first NCAA championship in any sport in Texas Tech history.

Besides responding to a growing population and economy, city leaders began to develop a new interest and pride in the history of Lubbock. All of a sudden, Lubbock seemed to become interested in itself as a city rather than as just an isolated place with some powerful and occasionally colorful people. In 1990 former city councilman Bob Nash was recognized as the city joined with Texas Tech University in dedicating the Bob Nash Interpretive Center of the Lubbock Lake Landmark. An enthusiastic local history buff and promoter, Nash had worked tirelessly to gain recognition for this significant archeological site and helped secure its designation as a National Historic landmark and state nature reserve. The small lake and its immediate environment continues as a significant international archeological dig, unearthing evidence that this lake has served as a vital human and animal water source for over 12,000 years, including the first site of the Anglo settlement in what is now Lubbock.

This new interest in the roots of Lubbock culture also led Patterson and city council colleagues to rethink their attitude toward the musical traditions of the city and the surrounding region. Since 1979 the city had acknowledged famous local and regional musicians through annual induction into the West Texas Walk of Fame, and it boasted a Grant Speed statue of Buddy Holly, but Lubbock music was not a dynamic part of community activities until the 1990s. Indeed, in 1980 famous Lubbock rock-and-roll star Joe Ely organized a rock festival on his own. Called the Tornado Jam and held at Buddy Holly Park on May 11, the rock concert commemorated the tenth anniversary of the 1970 Lubbock tornado and, through the location, acknowledged Lubbock's early rock-and-roll icon. The first year 8,000 rowdy music fans showed up. In 1981 the Tornado Jam drew 30,000 enthusiastic young participants, and in 1982 over 50,000 people descended on Lubbock to dance, sing, smoke marijuana, and drink every kind of liquor as they celebrated the live music of a vast docket of talented performers. Perhaps the Lubbock city council began to see the specter of Woodstock haunting the event. Certainly, it appeared to be a raucous, counterculture crowd. In every way it was a very unusual outburst of public exuberance for Lubbock, and the council choked. The Tornado Jam was refused a permit for 1983. Soon after, Joe Ely left Lubbock and settled in Austin, Texas, taking his talented musical cohort with him. A decade later the Lubbock city council of Patterson and Trejo began to think it might not be such a bad idea for Lubbock to become some kind of party town.

In 1991 David Langston began organizing Broadway Festivals to support a series of community events, with Fourth on Broadway becoming the most successful and quickly evolving into the largest free festival in Texas. This all-day, family-friendly Fourth of July occasion offered tens of thousands of participants ongoing entertainment through a kick-off parade, music venues, heritage events, street foods, and children's games, ending with an evening musical concert followed by a massive fireworks display. The event still exists today as a celebration of local talent, showcasing every kind of musical expression that Lubbock has to offer. As mayor, Langston also orchestrated the purchase of a large cache of Buddy Holly memorabilia. To display these valuable artifacts, the Lubbock city council unanimously secured and renovated the 1928 Fort Worth and Denver Railway Depot as the Buddy Holly Center, celebrating the life and times of

Buddy Holly and providing the city with a state-of-the-art fine-arts gallery. In 1988 the Lubbock city council invested in another city museum with the initial funding to establish Silent Wings at the old municipal airport. The Silent Wings Museum displays rare artifacts from the military-glider training school located in Lubbock during World War II. The Buddy Holly Center opened in 1999 under the mayoral leadership of Windy Sitton. The council also expanded this new focus on entertainment by designating the area surrounding this new facility as the Depot District.

Local musician and entrepreneur Don Caldwell played a significant role in promoting the Depot District and engaging the public in the extraordinary and long-ignored musical talents of Lubbock. He restored the 1942 Cactus Theater on what was then Avenue H, now Buddy Holly Avenue, and began booking live performances of famous local and regional musicians. To support featured performances, he organized and played saxophone in a talented house band that also celebrated regional musical traditions through its own concerts. Mayor Marc McDougal built on the development of the Depot District by enlisting the city council, with unanimous consent, to support a yearly music festival celebrating Buddy Holly's birthday. Don Caldwell organized these events, working with the city and through the strictures of Buddy Holly's widow, Maria Elena Holly, to celebrate the dynamic talents of the city, including, among many others, the Maines Brothers Band and the Joe Ely Band, brought back home to gain the respect they always deserved.

Patterson was gratified that the Eastside also received recognition for important contributions to the Lubbock music tradition. In 1999 sculptor and singer-songwriter Terry Allen created a bronze statue memorializing Christopher B. "Stubb" Stubblefield and dedicated it at the site of Stubb's Bar-B-Q on East Broadway. In the 1970s and through the early 1980s, Stubb brought Chicago blues musicians to his restaurant, hosted open-mic Sunday night jams, and nurtured a new generation of Lubbock musicians, including Joe Ely, Terry Allen, Jessie "Guitar" Taylor, and Jimmie Dale Gilmore. He often announced his musical events by advertising in the *Southwest Digest*. Stubb followed Joe Ely to Austin, where his restaurant and live-music venue lives on after his death, and his name is known nationwide through Stubb's Original and Spicy Barbecue Sauce, available in grocery stores everywhere.

After retiring from his position as principal of Dunbar Junior High in 1993, Virgil Johnson also joined in this new celebration of Lubbock music. He became "VJ the Deejay" for the reconstituted radio station KDAV, a legacy station located in the Depot District that helped celebrate and promote the music of West Texas from the 1950s. Johnson began performing again, singing his signature song "Tonight (Could Be the Night)" and other doo-wop favorites at events around Lubbock and the nation. In 2006 Virgil Johnson was inducted into the West Texas Walk of Fame with a ceremony that had become more elaborate as the music of the city gained significance to Lubbock citizens.[20]

Patterson supported city investment in Lubbock history and culture, plus new development activity, from annexation to paved roads to water mains to fire stations, ever moving south and west, but he was unable to put together a council coalition to help him bring new development to the northeast quadrant, although he certainly talked it up enough. Always a practical leader, he spent his time on the council concentrating on what he actually could build for his district.

In 1993 Patterson organized the committee headed by Joan Ervin to consider a name change for Quirt Avenue. She and her fellow committee members collected petition signatures requesting "quirt" be stricken from the city street sign language and received multicultural support. Irvin says of the effort, "The petition of signatures were red, white, black and blue, and that has not eroded any in this community. The celebration was unbelievable. It was truly tri-ethnic representation." The petition won unanimous council approval, and Irvin explains that naming the street Martin Luther King, Jr. Boulevard was not presented with the petition. It was secondary to eliminating that culturally charged term "quirt" from the Eastside environment, although Martin Luther King, Jr. Boulevard turned out to be the perfect name for this main artery through East Lubbock.[21]

In that same year a bond issue passed to finance a series of branch libraries, and Patterson made sure that one was located in the Eastside. In his honor the facility was named the T. J. Patterson Library. When the branch opened at 1836 Parkway Drive on December 6, 1995, Mayor Emanuel Cleaver of Kansas City, Missouri, was present as the keynote speaker to celebrate Patterson. Emanuel Cleaver and T. J. Patterson are cousins. Cleaver served on the city council of Kansas City for twelve years, as mayor of Kansas City for eight years, and since 2004 has represented Missouri's Fifth Congressional District, which includes Kansas City and most of Jackson County. In the 112th Congress, he was elected the chair of the Congressional Black Caucus. From 1972 until 2009, Cleaver also served as pastor of Saint James United Methodist Church in Kansas City. Like Patterson, Cleaver was born in Waxahachie and grew up in Wichita

Falls. The audience attending the ceremony was surprised when Mayor Cleaver announced the topic of his speech, "T. J. Patterson Is Good for Nothing." Surprise, however, turned to smiles when Cleaver explained that T. J. Patterson was the type of man who would go out of his way to do something for you without expecting anything in return. In 2003 Lubbock city councilman Victor Hernandez sponsored a unanimously adopted resolution to rename the library the Bobbie Gean and T. J. Patterson Library.[22]

In 1994 University Medical Center, the county-supported teaching hospital for the Texas Tech University Health Sciences Center, opened a neighborhood clinic at the historic Chatman Hospital just around the corner from Patterson's residence in Carver Heights. Through the efforts of Dr. Joseph Alvin Chatman's son Harold, his friends, and University Medical Center, the black hospital built in 1945 was totally renovated. The reopening of this medical facility was a boon to the community, as well as a symbol of all that had changed in Lubbock. In the early days, as in Wichita Falls, African Americans received medical treatment primarily in their homes. West Texas Hospital, located in downtown Lubbock, would not accept African Americans at all, and Katie Parks illustrates the point by recounting an incident from the 1940s. "An African American business man, Paul Hermanes, had an auto accident and was carried to West Texas Hospital because the ambulance driver thought he was Anglo. When his wife arrived to see him, the hospital found out he was an African American. He was dismissed immediately although he was in serious condition."[23]

Lubbock Sanitarium would admit African Americans but placed them in the basement near the garbage cans, with male and female patients separated by a sheet as a curtain. It was only when the Sisters of Saint Joseph established their Catholic hospital, Saint Mary of the Plains, in 1937, that blacks and Hispanics were offered complete hospital services. However, to better accommodate the needs of his patients, Dr. Joseph Alvin Chatman opened Chatman Hospital in the heart of the black community in 1945, no small feat given that city water mains were not extended to the Eastside or the Barrio until 1947. Desegregation diminished the need for a black hospital, and after Dr. Chatman's death in 1967, the hospital burned and remained only as a shell. The opening of the Chatman Community Health Clinic as a part of the vast medical network of the city was one more step in Patterson's dream of uniting all parts of Lubbock as one community. Today, Patterson's neighborhood is known as Chatman Hill.[24]

Patterson has always extolled the beauty and economic potential of the Eastside and in his role as city councilman, he made sure he gave full support to the Yellowhouse Canyon Lakes project. Now renamed the Jim Bertram Lake System, Canyon Lakes was an ambitious reclamation enterprise begun by the city right after the tornado. The plan created six lakes on the canyon edge of north and east Lubbock as part of the wastewater disposal system that also provided new outdoor recreational areas for the city. Five of these lakes are located in East Lubbock and serve the community as picnic sites, fishing spots, and natural beautification additions to the neighborhoods. One lake is the fulcrum of what has become known as Buddy Holly Park, the site of the infamous and spectacular Tornado Jams, and is located on the edge of the traditionally Hispanic area of town. The road winding through the Jim Bertram Lake System is now named Cesar E. Chavez Drive.

Patterson did all he could to nurture the promise of the lakes system and continued to dream of retail and residential development to follow, but the beauty of the area never seemed to be quite enough to shift development sensibilities. That changed when Mayor Marc McDougal joined with Patterson and Hernandez to put forth an initiative to encourage new construction in this most beautiful area of the city. In 2002 the Lubbock city council created the North and East Lubbock Community Development Corporation to support private development in the northeast quadrant of the city.

Mayor Marc McDougal was accustomed to looking eastward rather than westward. As development in southwest Lubbock went on its merry way, his real estate business, McDougal Companies, had turned its attention to the old, historic part of Lubbock. McDougal Companies is a family-owned and family-operated business. Marc McDougal is the son of company founder, Delbert McDougal. In 1998 Delbert McDougal took on the challenge of redeveloping the neighborhood of North Overton, the very first 1907 city annexation, two years before Lubbock was officially incorporated. Located between Texas Tech University and downtown, the neighborhood had fallen into deep disarray, a crime-ridden part of the city with only 3 percent owner occupancy. Through the resources of his company, Delbert McDougal determined to revitalize this 325-acre area as the largest privately funded urban development project in the nation. He proceeded by virtually razing the whole neighborhood and starting over, adding student apartment complexes, new homes, a new conference hotel, a Wal-Mart shopping center, and a number of other retail stores on the perimeter of the neighborhood. Even surprising himself, McDougal was able to renew much of the area by 2006, with a goal of completing all the finishing touches by 2016. The Lubbock city council embraced the Overton project with great enthusiasm and every municipal support available. City leaders were thrilled that this urban renewal project was putting North Overton back on the tax rolls and eliminating the chronic drug violence and prostitution that had plagued the old neighborhood.[25]

Interests in old Lubbock redevelopment had somehow trained McDougal's eye to look even past "the concrete curtain" of Interstate 27 into the northeast quadrant of the city and support the concerns of Patterson and Hernandez for the growth of their districts. Through the work of the North and East Lubbock Community Development Corporation, the Parkway shopping center on Parkway Drive was revitalized, and a new fire station stands on Martin Luther King, Jr. Boulevard (MLK). In 2005 Kent Hance built the Park Meadow apartment complex on the west side of MLK, and in 2006 Betenbaugh Homes built Kings Dominion on the east side of MLK, across the street from Estacado High School. This project was the first residential development in East Lubbock since 1954. The Courtyard at Kings Dominion has recently been added as a senior living facility. The area also gained the I-27 Industrial Park, which houses many companies plus the Lubbock branch of the Texas Department of Public Safety.

Finally, there was a beginning of significant new growth in East Lubbock, but Patterson did not get to experience these new developments as a Lubbock city councilman. In 2004 he lost his reelection bid to the council, beaten by Floyd Price. Price was the sixteenth black police officer in Lubbock and the second black police officer to retire from the Lubbock Police Department. During his long tenure with the force, Price was the first black officer to ride patrol in southwest Lubbock, the first to ride with a white officer, and the first to train a white officer. He was joined on the police force by black officers Fulton Berry and William Britt, and Price explains, "We were the first to patrol Lubbock. . . . We weren't confined to a certain part of our community. We were the first African Americans to have an integrated police department. We integrated the police department. The police department was segregated when we joined." Britt joined in 1963, Price in 1966, and Berry in 1969.

For thirteen years Price patrolled on a motorcycle and joined with Berry and Britt in the 1970s to host a Sunday afternoon radio show called the "Soul Patrol." The program helped keep the young people off the streets while they listened. "Soul Patrol" had a phone line for requests or just to talk, and the show built community trust in the police. "We were trying to bring the communication in, and make people come together," Price says. "Not only was there tensions with the races, but when we started Soul Patrol—that erased it." The trio even released a single, titled "Don't Knock the Cop." They sang backup, and Price's brother sang lead. "Soul Patrol" ran for five and a half years, and District 2 remembered the program and Price's years of outreach when he ran for the city council in 2004.[26]

Of course, Patterson was disappointed at the loss of his council seat, but he took the defeat philosophically. "I wish all of them well," he says. "I was a grateful winner, but I had to be a gracious loser. I'd be lying if I said it didn't bother me what happened, but I'm a realist. One and one is two. . . . I learned from an old banker named Wayne Finnell. He said, 'Let me tell y'all something. The sun's going to rise in the east with me or without me every morning.'" Finnell was president of Lubbock National Bank and president of the Lubbock Chamber of Commerce in 1970. He played a leading role in helping the city move forward after the tornado and obviously shared Patterson's sense of how a person fits into the grand scheme of things. "Any job, any opportunity to serve in any capacity is worthy of your pursuit," Patterson insists. "But in public service, you serve the public while understanding that the things you do during your time in office might not come to fruition for ten or twenty years, but at least you will have planted some seeds for that to happen. That's government."[27]

During his long tenure on the Lubbock city council, Patterson had gained a citywide reputation as a strong and respected leader, giving voice to the needs and concerns of the African American community and serving as an effective advocate for vulnerable citizens of every culture. He was admired for his negotiation skills, his deep commitment to his district, and his genuine affection for people. Mayor Windy Sitton served on the city council with Patterson from 1994 to 1996 and as Lubbock mayor from 1996 to 2002. She says of him, "I think he is an extremely good role model for not only African-American kids but for all kids because he is a man of character. He is a man of God. He lives his life that way, and he goes about life doing good for other people. He is very genuine. He is a genuine man whose heart is in the right place."[28]

On July 9, 2004, Lubbock Congressman Randy Neugebauer stepped up to the podium of the United States House of Representatives to pay tribute to Thomas James Patterson. Neugebauer had served on the Lubbock city council with Patterson from 1992 to 1998 and expressed his admiration for him in an *Avalanche-Journal* article: "T. J. is Randy Neugebauer's hero," he proclaimed. "I have known T. J. a number of years, all the way back to when I was at Texas Tech, and he was out there. . . . T. J. is a selfless public servant. He is always thinking about Lubbock and what's good for Lubbock. He is always interested in what's the right thing to do." Neugebauer became District 19 congressional district representative in 2003 and was proud to read the accomplishments of his colleague into the Congressional Record.[29]

> *"Mr. Speaker, I rise today in recognition of a good friend, T. J. Patterson, who this week, ended twenty years of service on Lubbock's City Council. T. J. served on ten city councils and under five different mayors.*
>
> *"I had the pleasure of serving with Councilman T. J. Patterson and what I learned in my six years in serving with T. J. is what most folks in Lubbock know, that he is a strong community leader and a tireless fighter for the values of the people he serves.*
>
> *"T. J. is a man of many firsts. After serving his country in Vietnam, T. J. became the first African American elected to the Lubbock City Council. He was also the first African American elected to be president of the Texas Municipal League. He founded the Texas Association of Black City Council Members and also the publication,* Southwest Digest.
>
> *"During his twenty years of service T. J. Patterson fought so hard for the things that matter to the citizens of Lubbock and Lubbock families: educating our kids and protecting Lubbock's youth from gangs and drugs.*
>
> *"The people in Lubbock and I are grateful for T. J. Patterson's tireless service to his community."*

United States Congressional Records, July 9, 2004
Congressman Randy Neugebauer

Patterson had become a recognized and much-admired leader throughout the city by the 1990s and was named by the *Avalanche-Journal* as one of the "outstanding Lubbock leaders" in 1999. The article quotes him as saying, "I've heard some folks say leaders are born. I don't know if I agree with that. You have to go through the muck and mire. It's thrust upon you, and you have to accept it when it's there, and it's a lonely position."[30] He shared his perspective on public service with the new District 1 councilman, Floyd Price. "All the folk that support you, that's great. Call them back next month, and they won't even show up. That's the human beast because people want to see instant things, and you don't see things instantaneously. It doesn't happen like that. It took twenty years to come over to the North and East Lubbock Development Program, twenty years."

After devoting most of his adult life to education and public service, Patterson was determined to spend most of his energies in the future on the promise of private development, bringing "roof tops" to the Eastside. "The city is a great city," he says. "I love Lubbock, but it's not the only play in town." Identifying more investors interested in developing the northeast quadrant was the new play he envisioned, and the *Southwest Digest* would be the vehicle for spreading the word. The *Southwest Digest* would also continue in its mission to build a strong voting constituency as a crucial force for neighborhood development. Patterson had always understood the power of the vote and insists, "You got to do it 24/7, instead of getting mad when it affects you. You got to keep on doing it. Keep on doing it, can't quit, can't get frustrated. Oh, yeah, you cry sometimes, but you can't quit. You can't quit. That's the problem." He points to the low voter turnout as a factor in his 2004 Lubbock city council loss, although many longtime political pundits contend that Patterson's ill health affected his campaigning and that that was the more likely factor.[31]

In April of 2004, Patterson suffered two strokes, and that physical crisis sapped his energies. While undergoing rehab on the damage, he noticed signs of the return of his childhood bout with polio. "You know polio will reoccur," he says. "That's a true statement. I didn't die, they said, because of prayer. They sewed my back to cardboard so I could breathe, and God let me live." Remembering his victory as a child, he determined to beat his old enemy the same way he had as a three-year-old, through prayer, healthy habits, and an indomitable spirit. Patterson returned to private life with the determination to renew his strengths and enjoy his partnership with Eddie Richardson as they planted new seeds through the *Southwest Digest*. He was also gratified to be surrounded by his close-knit family, which now included grandchildren and a great-grandchild.

By 2004 Bobbie had retired from her LISD position as a very successful counselor and diagnostician after forty years as a Lubbock educator. For her talents and commitment she had been recognized by the MLK Commemorative Council as Educator of the Year. She was also recognized as the United Juneteenth Commission of Lubbock Trendsetter and remained energetically involved in the activities of the East Lubbock community and her church. Bobbie still sang in the choir, served on church boards, and engaged in the broader church community.

The Patterson family was always actively involved in church, with T. J. serving as Sunday school teacher, superintendent, and leader of the Bethel

AME Boy Scout troop, "one of the biggest packs in Lubbock," says Evangelist Mona Cleveland Shaw. Bethel AME Reverend Sonia J. Scott calls Patterson "a gentle giant" and praises him for his love of God and the church he has served for over fifty-five years.[32] The Patterson children were deeply influenced by their parents' faith. They have embraced a Christian mission and carried on the family tradition of personal engagement in the church, confirming the advice from Proverbs 22:6, "Train up a child in the way he should go; even when he is old he will not depart from it."

Guided by the gospel, Councilman Patterson extended his concern for the protection and guidance of his own children to all God's children. His many antidrug marches were conducted to save young people from harm, and as a city councilman he gave strong support to the city's juvenile curfew ordinance that is renewed every three years. The curfew requires that young people under the age of sixteen must not be out in public places without adult supervision from 11:00 p.m. to 6:00 a.m., Sunday through Thursday. On the weekend the curfew starts at midnight. Parents are held responsible for their children's whereabouts with a fine, if the curfew is broken. Patterson never hesitates to insist that children need a strong and steady adult hand in their raising, a hand that extends to their back side sometimes, even in public places. It is that combination of Christian upbringing and loving parental discipline that has shaped the three Patterson children and kept the family close.[33]

After attending Texas Tech University for two years, then moving to Cincinnati, Avis Elise returned to Lubbock to build her career working for the Water Department of the city of Lubbock and has remained deeply involved in her church. Like Bobbie, she is very musical. "I do sing and play the piano for my church," she says. "I am a worship leader at my church, and I also help out another church. I'm helping out with their ministry, to help get them started with praise and worship." Her son, Marcus Jerrod Williams, graduated from The Ohio State University with a bachelor's degree in psychology and a master's degree in both human resources and higher education; he is employed as a human resources director with Exxon Mobil in Houston. He and his wife, Emmanuella, have a son, Nathan, giving Patterson his only great-grandson.

Avis has always taught piano and voice lessons, and a stint with a furniture store inspired another side business in interior design. "Actually, short term, I am trying to build more knowledge in the business. . . . I hope, in time, to have my own company. I really have a passion for interior decorating." However, her most abiding passion is her church work. "I don't know where I see myself in the future, but . . . I am a worship leader at my church, so I'm very much into church. So, I take it very seriously and also . . . the things God has promised me and shown me. I will be traveling—city, state, and nation—to teach about worship and whatever He has me to do. That's what I want to set my goal for, to be in Christ and to honor His kingdom. . . . I hope to have my own business and be involved in ministry." She also seems to understand her love and respect for her father, from childhood on, in spiritual terms. "I knew there was some type of favor on him," she says. "There was a special calling on his life, and probably at the time, I couldn't put it into words that I'm putting it into now, but now that I think about it, he was a very giving person. He would give anything he could to help anybody, so, yes, I did feel like he was very special." [34]

Tommy Patterson is also deeply engaged in the Christian community. He serves as the Pastor for Elm Grove Missionary Baptist Church in Fort Worth, Texas. He is also the first African American to hold the office of senior assistant city attorney of Fort Worth. Tommy and his wife, Ursula, have two teenage children, Thomas Jefferson Paterson III and Lauren Elise Patterson.

After receiving his undergraduate degree from North Texas State University, Reverend T. J. Patterson, Jr., received his doctor of jurisprudence from Thurgood Marshall School of Law on the campus of Texas Southern University in Houston, Texas. This highly acclaimed law school was originally the very one that the Texas legislature had cobbled together in 1947 to make a law school on the campus of the brand-new Texas State University for the Negroes in an attempt to keep Texas segregated and Heman Marion Sweatt out of the University of Texas. The names have changed, the resources have changed, and the quality of the programs has changed profoundly, serving as a testament to human ingenuity and a talent for turning a racial liability into an educational opportunity.

Soon after graduating from North Texas in 1984, Tommy went to work as a lobbyist for the Texas secretary of state and discovered his father's election was news all across the state. When he enrolled in Thurgood Marshall School of Law, he found his father's reputation extended to the law school as well. "Even down in Houston, there were folks down there, folks he's met," Tommy says. "And then, when I graduated from law school and went to work for different politicians around the state, they always talked about my father and [how] he helped them and how he gave and cared about people." Patterson has had a great influence on his son, and as a pastor Tommy guides young people by following in his father's footsteps. "He always wanted to make sure that the young people knew that they were somebody," Tommy says. "Now I carry that on myself when I talk to young folks."[35]

Shelia returned to Lubbock after her education at the North Texas State University with a degree in radio, television, and film. She spent some years moving around the local radio world and explains the limitations on her mass-media career. "The thing of it was, I was kind of rebellious, and my dad tells this story: 'Every time I saw you, I never knew what your hair was going to look like.' I had this thing where I liked to try different things with my hair. I'd go blonde, and I'd do cuts and stuff, and I was told that there was something that stood out about me and my presence, my appearance. That was probably one of the things that kept me out of television, so I did radio."

Shelia is married to Shaun Harris and has two children. Her son, Zarrieus, received his engineering degree from Texas A&M University and is employed at TTI in Riverside, California. He also serves as a minister. Daughter Asya earned her license in cosmetology, receiving her state license while a senior at Monterey High School. Shelia just retired as the assistant supervisor for Lubbock's Juvenile Justice Center, where she served as probation supervisor at the Thirty-fourth Street annex, which includes a youth center. "I didn't go to school for that," Shelia explains. "I think it's my calling. I finally stopped long enough to realize that this is what I'm supposed to do."[36]

Patterson enjoyed being home, getting more involved with his family, and working with Eddie Richardson on issues at the *Southwest Digest*. It was a presidential election year in 2004, and both were involved in Democratic Party politics. There was also new hope on the horizon for their community, and Patterson went to work on private investment, or what he calls "the mighty ocean," for the Eastside. Choosing yet another earthy metaphor, he says, "Little threads of cotton make big ropes; got to know how to use it though. We must not use it on ourselves. Got to, then we can grow. Then you get so-called power. Then folks pay attention to you. Okay, now we got to use what we got."[37] Patterson and Richardson continued to keep each other company with great pleasure and were willing to admit that, as the years rolled by, their newspaper duties were becoming more challenging. "Now, we're getting to the age, hell, we're getting too old to do this stuff," Patterson confesses. "But it's too good to let go. It's just now getting there. . . . That's nothing but the goodness of God." He sums up:

"But through it all, I wouldn't exchange none of it, my brother. I wouldn't exchange none of it. Nobody will destroy my joy, nobody."[38]

While Patterson had returned to a joyful private life and was generally out of the public eye, the people didn't forget his valuable contributions to the community. Fay Brown, founder and CEO of "Each One, Reach One" in Lubbock, announced the establishment of the $10,000 T. J. and Bobbie Patterson Scholarship Endowment with the Texas Tech Alumni Association. The first scholarship was presented on March 21, 2009. That same year, cousins T. J. Patterson and Emanuel Cleaver were added to the Freedman Memorial in Waxahachie, Texas, with the titles "T. J. Patterson—Mayor Pro Tem" and "Emanuel Cleaver—US Congress." Patterson was also named by the Texas House of Representatives as an "outstanding Texan who has long distinguished his professional achievements and his many years of community leadership." In 2011 Eric Strong organized a committee to coordinate the T. J. Patterson Art Roast to raise more funds for the T. J. and Bobbie Patterson Scholarship Endowment and also help support the establishment of the Caviel African American Museum and Cultural Center.

The event was a gala affair held at the Civic Center banquet hall on Sunday, October 23, 2011. More than 450 people gathered to celebrate the contributions of the Pattersons. The roasters included the CEO of the Price Group and author of this book, Phil Price; the Lubbock Chamber of Commerce president, Irasema Velasquez; Fort Worth city councilman Frank Moss; the executive director of the National Girl's Self Esteem Program, Candida Johnson; and Patterson's cousin and the president of the Congressional Black Caucus, Emanuel Cleaver. Texas Tech Chancellor Kent Hance joined in the roast by video. Jeff Klotzman, anchor of Fox 34, served as emcee. Many humorous stories were told but very few were roast-worthy. The presenters were full of praise for Patterson's many civic achievements and lauded him for his kindness and his support of young people. In his reply to the toasts and the celebration of his life, Patterson reminded the audience in his strongest gospel style, "We do more than occupy space. We're God's creatures."

The banquet room was lined with visual art. There was much talk about Eric Strong's effort to establish the new Caviel African American Museum and Cultural Center to be housed in the Billie and Alfred Caviel Pharmacy at 1719 Avenue A, where the Caviels had offered their special services to the Lubbock African American community for fifty years. Located on the edge of the historic Chatman Hill neighborhood, the museum is dedicated to a celebration of the arts and the story of resilience that the Lubbock black community has to share.

Following the roast the audience was entertained with the music and dance of a series of distinguished black performing artists who all had their roots in West Texas. Opera star Terry Cook, who flew to Lubbock from New York City; jazz saxophonist Tom Braxton; professional ballerina NaTalia Johnson; and Jerome Bell, who was a 2011 finalist on "American Idol," all shared their exceptional talents with the crowd to great appreciation and applause. There was, however, also an elegiac edge to the evening. Virgil Johnson was on the program to perform but at the last minute found he was too ill to sing for his old, dear friend. In his final years Johnson suffered from a series of strokes and passed away in 2013, followed by great tributes from the community for his many gifts to Lubbock. Eddie Richardson had died at his home on December 10, 2010, leaving Patterson to soldier on at the *Southwest Digest* and for the rest of his life without his fiery, closest friend of more than four decades. Richardson was seventy-four years old and was honored at the Juneteenth Celebration that following June 19, 2011. "We couldn't say T. J. without mentioning Eddie Richardson in the same sentence," Velasquez said at the roast. Indeed, what a team they were, each in his own way, fighting for racial justice and opportunity through every avenue they could possibly find. Patterson himself had been under the strain of illness, and in an *Avalanche-Journal* article anticipating the roast, reporter Irie Price wrote, "The first black and longest-serving city councilman says he's got a thick skin, toughened after surviving two strokes and his bouts with diabetes and high blood pressure." He was also fighting post-polio syndrome and walked with difficulty, often needing to lean on a cane, desk, or chair to move around his office. In this public appearance he brought his rolling walker to greet the evening's audience. "I'm just blessed to be here," he told the reporter.[39]

The most disturbing issue of this gala evening was Bobbie's health. She was in treatment for cancer but displayed her characteristic charm and good spirits with the shadow of a threatening illness looming over her. No one would have guessed, but for those who knew, it was a poignant performance as she responded to the praise and exuberance of the crowd. Bobbie Gean Bailey Patterson died less than three months later on January 13, 2012. She was seventy-three years old. Her funeral was heralded as a "home-coming celebration," paying great tribute to this devout woman of God and devoted wife, mother, and teacher.[40]

In a 1999 *Avalanche-Journal* article, reporter Ray Westbrook asked Patterson whether there was anything besides service to others that he wanted for himself, and Patterson answered with a scenario on aging. "One day," he said, "when I can't see no more like I once did, or walk like I once did, when I can't get around and arthritis has got me in the arm and the leg, then I will be on the front porch and some young kids will come by. They will be saying, 'There's old man Patterson on the porch. He can't do what he used to do; he can't get around. Let's go buy him a Coke and talk to him.' To me, that's a great thing. I think that's what I want to do, just to be there to help somebody. All these other things will pass away; they will pass by; they won't mean nothin'. But how I treat my fellow man is what's going to really count."[41]

From 2010 to 2013, Patterson was left with the loneliness of great loss as his oldest friends and loving wife passed away, but even with all the sorrow, he was not just "old man Patterson" sitting on that front porch quite yet. To this day he continues to produce an issue of the *Southwest Digest* every week, with 4,000 copies still being inserted in the Friday edition of the Lubbock *Avalanche-Journal.* He still has a great interest in Lubbock city government and serves on the Public Transit Advisory Board, keeping a close eye on municipal services to the Eastside. In May of 2015, he was recognized, once again, by the Texas legislature for his years of public service, and in 2016 he traveled to Austin to celebrate the thirtieth anniversary of the Texas Association of Black City Council Members, the organization he founded during his first years on the Lubbock city council. The T. J. Patterson, Sr., Golf Classic is still an elemental part of the annual meeting, and in 2016 the event raised almost $35,000 for scholarships. Patterson says of the organization, "We always do the best we can for the future. You don't do it for right now. You do it for the things coming afterwards."[42]

The greatest joy of the year 2016 came with the election of Shelia Patterson Harris to the Lubbock city council in Patterson's old seat, as representative for District 2. Her candidacy caught him by surprise. "I didn't think she was gonna run for no office," Patterson says. "I was surprised when she did that. I didn't comment. I said, 'Jesus Christ, look at her.' I didn't know what to say, but I was happy." Like her father that very first time in 1984, Shelia ran against four other contenders, Tiger Pratt, Gordon Harris, Jared Hall, and Christopher Moore. But unlike her father, she couldn't avoid a runoff. Fortunately, she had a steady and knowledgeable advisor to help guide her campaign, a father who knew more about the people and the needs of District 2 than anyone else around. She won the runoff against lawyer Jared Hall and took office in July 2016, along with Juan Chadis, the new councilman for District 1, who also won in a runoff election.[43] Together they serve the northeast quadrant, and Shelia indicates she is ready to lead, like her father, with passion. She plans to "start up from where he left off and continue to move forward," she tells an *Avalanche-Journal* reporter, Austin Kemker. "It's going to be a difficult task but anything is. And anything that isn't difficult for you is sometimes not worth taking on. I know it's going to take building relationships . . . for some of the additional things to take place in District 2 and in the city of Lubbock. Because I often say that if there's one area in the city that's not thriving, then there's no way we can say the city's thriving." Patterson offers his daughter encouragement and some words of wisdom. "When you fall, we'll help pick you up," he promises her. "I'm watching you. I know where you live; I have your phone number; . . . the children are watching you. They're watching everything that you do. They've got an eye on you. The legislation that you pass won't affect you. It'll affect those children over there."

Shelia can expect much advice and encouragement from her father, and he can expect to feel great pride in her achievements. They both value service to others and understand the slow time of successful public works. The election of Shelia Patterson Harris brings a special glow to all the tributes that Patterson has received. His youngest daughter has taken on his civic mission and will bring her unbounded energies and ideas to building a better community. Her election adds new depth to his legacy. Now, when he finally gets around to sitting on his front porch, waving at the kids when they walk by, they might say, "That's old Mr. Patterson. He's the father of our councilwoman. He made a difference and so does she. That family sure knows how to bring some kindling to the fire."

Notes

Chapter 1

1. Lubbock City Council Minutes, April 12, 1984. Election results: T. J. Patterson, 1,281; Gilbert Herrera, 666; Jim Taylor, 277; Roy C. Jones, 133; Pedro (Pete) Mora, 84.
2. Daniel H. Benson Records, 1959–1984, Texas Tech University Southwest Collection/Special Collections, Reel 3: Brief to the United States Court of Appeals for the Fifth Circuit, 1979. See also, Roger Schaefer, "Law and Politics in Lubbock: 1945 to the Present," in *Lubbock from Town to City*, ed. Lawrence L. Graves (Lubbock: West Texas Museum Association, 1986), 143–47.
3. Steve Poole, "Diversity in City Leadership Still a Concern Thirty Years Later," *Lubbock Avalanche-Journal*, July 6, 2015.
4. *Southwest Digest*, March 1–7, 1984.
5. Texas Tech University Southwest Collection/Special Collections, digital collection of *Lubbock Digest* and *Southwest Digest*, 1977–1984.
6. Ibid.
7. T. J. Patterson and Eddie Richardson interview by Eric Strong, "The History of the *Southwest Digest*," October 1, 2007.
8. Eddie Richardson interview by Phil Price, January 31, 2009.
9. T. J. Patterson and Eddie Richardson interview by Eric Strong, "The History of *Southwest Digest*," October 1, 2007.
10. According to the official city of Lubbock website in 2016, District 2 has a population of 32,800, with a black population of 28.7 percent or 9,413 people. Traditional East Lubbock only includes precincts 6, 20, and 40, the area of District 2 that functions as a small community and is referred to as the Eastside. http://www.ci.lubbock.tx.us.
11. Eddie Richardson interview by Phil Price, March 2, 2010.
12. T. J. Patterson and Eddie Richardson interview by Eric Strong, "The History of the *Southwest Digest*," October 1, 2007.

13. “Bishop College,” Texas State Historical Association, http://www.tshaonline.org/handbook/online/article/kbb11.
14. T. J. Patterson interview by Phil Price, September 20, 2013, with email follow-up on September 21, 2013.
15. Virgil Johnson interview by Phil Price, January 15, 2009.
16. E. J. Donaldson interview by Phil Price, May 18, 2009.
17. “Virgil Johnson,” Wikipedia. http://en.wikipedia.org/ wiki/Virgil_Johnson_(Singer).
18. Virgil Johnson interview by Phil Price, January 15, 2009.
19. Katie Parks, *Remember When?: a History of African Americans in Lubbock, Texas*, (Lubbock: Texas Tech University Press, 1999), 104.
20. “Bishop College R.I.P.?” *D Magazine* (August 1987): 4.
21. “America’s Civil Rights Timeline,” International Civil Rights Center and Museum, Greensboro, North Carolina, https://www.sitinmovement.org/history/americancivil-rights-timeline.asp.
22. “The Negro Holocaust: Lynching and Race Riots in the United States, 1880–1950,” Yale–New Haven Teachers Institute, http://www.yaleedu/ynhti/curriculum/units/1979/2/79.02.04.html.
23. “America’s Civil Rights Timeline.”
24. “They Changed the World,” selected stories from the *Montgomery Advertiser* archives, http://www.montgomeryboycott.com/archived-articles.
25. T. J. Patterson interview by Phil Price, September 20, 2013.
26. “America’s Civil Rights Timeline.”
27. Donald Seals, Jr., “The Wiley-Bishop Student Movement: A Case Study in the 1960 Civil Rights Sit-ins,” *Southwestern Historical Quarterly* 106, no. 3 (January 2003): 418–40. See also “Black Students Sit-in for US Civil Rights, Marshall, Texas, 1960,” Global Movement Action Database, http://invdatabase.swarthmore.edu/content/black-student-sot-us-civil-rights-marshall-texas-1960.
28. “Marshall, Texas,” Wikipedia, https://en.wikipedia.org/wiki/Marshall_Texas.
29. T. J. Patterson interview by Phil Price, August 22, 2008.
30. Bill Moyers, “Marshall, Texas; Marshall, Texas,” A Second Look. Moyers & Company, 1984, http://billmoyers.com/content/second-look-marshall-texas.
31. Seals, “Wiley-Bishop Student Movement.”
32. T. J. Patterson interview by Pamela Brink, May 15, 2016.
33. Moyers, “Marshall, Texas.”
34. Seals, “Wiley-Bishop Student Movement.”
35. Bishop College R.I.P.?” See also “Negro College Fund President,” *New York Times*, March 28, 1975.

36. Moyers, "Marshall, Texas."
37. "America's Civil Rights Timeline."
38. T. J. Patterson interview by Daniel Sanchez, Texas Tech University Southwest Collection/Special Collections, July 26, 2004.
39. Jon Kutnes, Jr., "Swift and Company," Handbook of Texas Online, September 4, 2013, http://www.tshaonline.org/handbook/online/article/dis02.
40. T. J. Patterson interview by Daniel Sanchez, Texas Tech University Southwest Collection/Special Collections, July 26, 2004.
41. T. J. Patterson interview by Phil and Victoria Price, January 24, 2014.

Chapter 2

1. T. J. and Bobbie Patterson interview by Phil Price, April 13, 2009.
2. "*The Call* (Kansas City)," Wikipedia. http://en.wikipedia.org. "The History of the *Kansas City Call*," Black Archives of Mid-America in Kansas City, http://blackarchives.org.
3. T. J. and Bobbie Patterson interview by Phil Price, April 13, 2009.
4. "African Methodist Episcopal Church," Wikipedia, http://en.wikipedia.org. "Our History," Official Website of the African Methodist Episcopal Church, http://ame-church.com.
5. T. J. and Bobbie Patterson interview by Phil Price, April 13, 2009.
6. Parks, *Remember When?*, 48.
7. Ibid., 28.
8. Ibid. 185–86.
9. T. J. and Bobbie Patterson interview by Phil Price, April 13, 2009.
10. Robert L. Foster and Alwyn Barr, "Black Lubbock," in *West Texas Historical Association Year Book* (1978): 24–25.
11. Roger Schaefer, "Law and Politics in Lubbock: 1945 to the Present," in *Lubbock from Town to Gown*," Lawrence L. Graves, ed. (West Texas Museum Association, 1986), 151–61.
12. Merton L. Dillon, "Religion in Lubbock," in *A History of Lubbock, Part Three*, Lawrence L. Graves, ed. (West Texas Museum Association, 1961) 497.
13. Mike Cockran and John Lumpkin, *West Texas: A Portrait of Its People and Their Raw and Wondrous Land*, (Texas Tech University Press, 1999), 36–38.
14. Ibid.
15. T. J. Patterson interview by Phil Price, August 22, 2008.
16. Naomi Rogers, "Race and the Politics of Polio: Warm Springs, Tuskegee, and the March of Dimes," *American Journal of Public Health* (May 2007), www.ncbi.nih.gov.
17. T. J. Patterson interview by Phil Price, August 22, 2008.

18. Beth Sokol, "Fear of Polio in the 1950s," *The Beat Begins: America in the 1950s*. Honors College at the University of Maryland, College Park, 1997.
19. Skip Watson interview by Phil Price, December 12, 2008.
20. "Polio," Wikipedia, http://en.wikipedia.org.
21. T. J. Patterson interview by Phil Price, August 22, 2008.
22. Randy Lewis, "My Hometown," Nogwog: No Greatness Without Goodness, http://nogwog.com/my-hometown. May 23, 2016.
23. T. J. Patterson interview by Phil Price, August 22, 2008.
24. E. J. Donaldson interview by Phil Price, May 18, 2009.
25. T. J. Patterson interview by Phil Price, August 22, 2008.
26. Bobbie and T. J. Patterson interview by Phil Price, April 12, 2009.
27. E. J. Donaldson interview by Phil Price, May 18, 2009.
28. Parks, *Remember When?*. 39–40.
29. E. J. Donaldson interview by Phil Price, May 18, 2009.
30. Bobbie and T. J. Patterson interview by Phil Price, April 13, 2009.
31. T. J. Patterson interview by Phil Price, August 22, 2008.
32. Ibid.

Chapter 3

1. Bobbie Patterson interview with Phil Price, January 13, 2012.
2. T. J. Patterson interview with Daniel Sanchez, Texas Tech University Southwest Collection/Special Collections July 26, 2004.
3. "Harry S. Truman Museum and Library," http://www.trumanlibrary.org.
4. Raymond Arsenault, *Freedom Riders: 1961 and the Struggle for Racial Justice* (Oxford University Press, 2006).
5. Don Bohning, *The Castro Obsession: US Covert Operations against Cuba, 1959–1965*, (Washington, DC: Potomac Books, 2005).
6. Thomas Adams Upchurch, *Race Relations in the United States, 1960–1980* (Westport, CT: Greenwood Press, 2008).
7. T. J. Patterson interview with Daniel Sanchez, Texas Tech University Southwest Collection/Special Collections, July 26, 2004.
8. Bobbie Patterson interview with Phil Price, January 13, 2012.
9. E. J. Donaldson interview with Phil Price, May 18, 2009.
10. T. J. and Bobbie Patterson interview with Phil Price, April 13, 2009.
11. T. J. Patterson interview with Daniel Sanchez, Texas Tech University Southwest Collection/Special Collections, July 26, 2004.
12. "The Vietnam War," The History Place, http://www.historyplace.com/unitedstates/vietnam/index-1945-html.
13. T. J. Patterson interview with Daniel Sanchez, Texas Tech University Southwest Collection/Special Collections, July 26, 2004.

14. Seth Jacobs, *Cold War Mandarin: Ngo Dinh Diem and the Origins of America's War in Vietnam, 1950–1963* (Lanham, MD: Rowman & Littlefield, 2006).
15. Edward Miller, *Misalliance: Ngo Dinh Diem, the United States, and the Fate of South Vietnam* (Harvard University Press, 2013).
16. T. J. Patterson interview with Daniel Sanchez, Texas Tech University Southwest Collection/Special Collections, July 26, 2004.
17. Andrew Wiest, *The Vietnam War* (Rosen Publishing, 2009).
18. "Hearts and minds" was a term used repeatedly by President Lyndon B. Johnson to refer to the strategy of counterinsurgency in the Vietnam War. *Hearts and Minds* is also a 1974 documentary film on the Vietnam War directed by Peter Davis, based on a quotation from President Johnson, "the ultimate victory will depend on the hearts and minds of the people who actually live out there." It was chosen as Best Documentary Feature at the 1975 Academy Awards.
19. Wiest, *Vietnam War.*
20. Ibid.
21. T. J. Patterson interview with Daniel Sanchez, Texas Tech University Southwest Collection/Special Collections, July 26, 2004.
22. T. J. and Bobbie Patterson interview by Phil Price, April 12, 2009.
23. Avis Elise Patterson interview by Phil Price, April 8, 2009.
24. T. J. Patterson, Jr., interview by Phil Price, March 3, 2008.
25. Shelia Patterson Harris interview by Phil Price, April 14, 2009.
26. T. J. Patterson interview by Phil Price, August 22, 2008.
27. Shelia Patterson Harris interview by Phil Price, April 14, 2009.
28. T. J. Patterson, Jr., interview by Phil Price, March 3, 2008.
29. Avis Elise Patterson interview by Phil Price, April 8, 2009.
30. T. J. Patterson, Jr., interview by Phil Price, March 3, 2008.
31. Shelia Patterson Harris interview by Phil Price, April 14, 2009.
32. John A. Andrew, *Lyndon Johnson and the Great Society* (Chicago: I. R. Dee, 1998).
33. "Head Start (program)," https://en/wikipedia.org/wiki/Head_Start_(program).
34. T. J. Patterson interview by Daniel Sanchez, Texas Tech University Southwest Collection/Special Collections, July 26, 2004.
35. Marshall Kaplan and Peggy L. Cuciti, *The Great Society and Its Legacy: Twenty Years of US Social Policy* (Durham, NC: Duke University Press, 1986).

Chapter 4

1. "Vietnam War Draft," http://thevietnamwar.info/vietnam-war-draft.
2. "The Vietnam War and the Draft," and John Sibley Butler, "African Americans

in the Vietnam War," from *The Oxford Companion to American Military History* (Oxford University Press, 1999).

3. "Martin Luther King, Jr., Speaks Out Against the War, April 4, 1967," This Day in History, http://www.history.com/this-day-in-history/martin-luther-king-jr-speaks-out-against-the-war.
4. T. J. Patterson interview by Phil Price, August 22, 2008.
5. Ibid.
6. "Lucille Sugar Barton Graves," Notable Women from Texas Tech University, http://swco.ttu.edu/university_archive/ttuwomen4.html.
7. Jane Gilmore Rushing and Kline A. Nall, *Evaluation of a University: Texas Tech's First Fifty Years* (Austin, TX: Madrona Press, 1975), 123.
8. "White-washed History," *Southwest Digest*, February 25, 1982.
9. "Graves, Lucille Sugar Barton," Texas State Historical Association, http://tshaonline.org/handbook/online/articles/fgrao.
10. Virgil Johnson interview with Phil Price, January 15, 2009.
11. "NAACP Legal History," http://www.naacp.org/pages/naacp-legal-history.
12. Gary M. Lavergne, *Before Brown: Heman Marion Sweatt, Thurgood Marshall, and the Long Road to Justice* (Austin: University of Texas Press, 2010).
13. "Booker T. Washington High School Reunion, Wichita Falls, Tx," CNN iReport, http://ireport.cnn.com/doc. See also Kyle Egan, "Segregation Era Students Recall Days at Midwestern," *Wichitan*, April 17, 2012.
14. "Atwell, William Hawley" Handbook of Texas Online, Texas State Historical Association, http://tshaonline.org/handbook/online/articles/fat05.
15. Egan, "Segregation Era Students."
16. T. J. Patterson interview by Pamela Brink, July 26, 2016.
17. "*Brown v. Board*: Timeline of School Integration in the US," Teaching Tolerance, http://www.tolerance.org/magazine/number-25-spring-2004/feature/brown-v-board-timeline-school-integration-us.
18. T. J. Patterson interview by Phil and Victoria Price, January 27, 2014.
19. C. Lynn Ainsworth, "Education and Medicine," in *Lubbock: From Town to Gown*, Lawrence Graves, ed., Museum Journal 23 (1986): 251
20. Jim Barlow, "Destruction of Homes Brought End of Segregation across City," *Lubbock Avalanche-Journal*, May 6, 1990.
21. James E. Jonish, "Population Growth and Expansion," *Lubbock: From Town to Gown.* Lawrence L. Graves, ed. Museum Journal 23 (1986): 114.
22. T. J. Patterson interview by Phil Price, August 22, 2008.
23. Doug Hensley, "A Growing Impact: City's Hispanics Have Come a Long Way from When Avenue H Was About as Far as We Could Go," *Lubbock Avalanche-Journal, The Lubbock Centennial*, 1909–2009, http://www.lubbockcentennial.com.

24. T. J. Patterson interview by Phil Price, August 22, 2008.
25. Ainsworth, "Education and Medicine," 252.
26. "Joan Ervin," *Lubbock Avalanche-Journal, Lubbock Centennial.*
27. Parks, *Remember When?*, 102.
28. Doug Hensley, "Lessons Well Learned," *Lubbock Avalanche-Journal, Lubbock Centennial.*
29. Doug Hensley, "Single Member Districts Benefitted LISD," *Lubbock Avalanche-Journal*, July 6, 2008.
30. Shelia Patterson Harris interview by Phil Price, April 14, 2009.
31. Pamela Brink, Cindy Martin, and Daniel Sánchez, *Lubbock* (Charleston, SC: Arcadia, 2013), 102 and 114.
32. Shelia Patterson Harris interview by Phil Price, April 14, 2009.
33. "Lubbock School Districts' Desegregation Case Helped Shape Solid Foundation for Students," *Lubbock Avalanche-Journal*, October 19, 2008.
34. Doug Hensley, "Dunbar More Than a Building to Community," *Lubbock Avalanche-Journal, Lubbock Centennial.*
35. Ibid.
36. Parks, *Remember When?*, 39.
37. "Dunbar Middle School," http://dunbar.lubbockisd.org/pages/dunbarcollege-prep.
38. "Dunbar High's 1965 State Champs Lived through Segregation with Pride, Unity," *Redraiders Texas Tech University Sports*, 1–9, http://redraidders.com.
39. "Council to Get Rid of 83-Year-Old Ordinance Defining Segregation," KCBD News Channel 11 Lubbock, http://www.kcbd.com.
40. "Wounds That Didn't Heal: Segregation in Lubbock," Mr. Lubbock, January 17, 2016, http://www.misterlubbock.com.
41. Hank Murphy, "LISD Learns from Desegregation Case," *Lubbock Avalanche-Journal*, April 25, 1999, http://lubbockonline.com.
42. Doug Hensley, "A Growing Impact," *Lubbock Avalanche-Journal, Lubbock Centennial.*
43. Linda Kane, "Judge Who Ordered Integration of Lubbock Schools Dies," *Amarillo Globe-News*, October 4, 2000, http://amarillo.com.
44. T. J. Patterson interview by Phil Price, April 22, 2008.
45. Doug Hensley, "A Growing Impact," *Lubbock Avalanche-Journal, Lubbock Centennial.*
46. Eddie Richardson interview by Phil Price, January 31, 2009.
47. "Eddie Price Richardson, Jr., Texas Online Handbook of Texas, https://tsha-online.org/handbook/online/articles/fri67.
48. "Juneteenth," Wikipedia, https://www.en.wikipedia.org.

49. Doug Hensley, "A Growing Impact," *Lubbock Avalanche-Journal, Lubbock Centennial.*
50. Eddie Richardson interview by Phil Price, January 31, 2009.

Chapter 5

1. T. J. Patterson interview by Daniel Sanchez, Texas Tech University Southwest Collections/Special Collections, July 26, 2004.
2. Alan Henry interview by Phil Price, January 30, 2009.
3. T. J. Patterson interview by Phil Price, January 23, 2009.
4. Ibid.
5. T. J. Patterson interview by Daniel Sanchez, Texas Tech University Southwest Collections/Special Collections, July 26, 2004.
6. Maggie Trejo interview by Phil Price, February 2, 2009.
7. James E. Jonish, "Population Growth and Expansion," 114.
8. Doug Hensley "A Growing Impact," *Lubbock Avalanche-Journal, Lubbock Centennial.*
9. "A Father to Many Lubbockites, Richard Lopez Dies at 74," *Lubbock Avalanche-Journal*, June, 20, 2008, http://www.lubbockonline.com.
10. Maggie Trejo interview by Phil Price, February 2, 2009.
11. Alan Henry interview by Pamela Brink, June 26, 2016.
12. Ibid.
13. Ray Westbrook, "Martin Luther King's Birthday to Involve Citywide Celebration," *Lubbock Avalanche-Journal*, January 16, 1997, http://www.lubbockonline.com.
14. T. J. Patterson interview by Phil Price, August 22, 2008.
15. "Texas Municipal League," TSHA Online Handbook of Texas, http://www.tshaonline.org.
16. T. J. Patterson interview by Phil Price, August 22, 2008.
17. Maggie Trejo interview by Phil Price, February 2, 2009.
18. Ray Westbrook, "Strong Beliefs Lead Trejo to Improve the Community Gracefully," *Lubbock Avalanche-Journal*, http://www.lubbockonline.com.
19. Paul H. Carlson and Donald R. Abbe, *The Centennial History of Lubbock: Hub City of the Plains* (Virginia Beach, VA: Donning Co., 2008), 125–65.
20. Ibid.
21. Ray Westbrook, "A Promising Road: City Unites to Change Street Name," *Lubbock Avalanche-Journal*, January 17, 1999, http://www.lubbockonline.com.
22. "Emanuel Cleaver," Wikipedia, http://www.en.wikipedia.org.
23. Parks, *Remember When?*, 155–56.
24. Ibid.

25. Carlson and Abbe, *Centennial History of Lubbock*, 125–65.
26. Parks, *Remember When?*, 189–91. Henry Ramos, "Councilman Price Remaining Member of "Soul Patrol," http://www.fox34.com.
27. Ray Westbrook, "Paterson's [sic] Years of Service in Public Eye Have Made Him a Hero to Many," *Lubbock Avalanche-Journal*, May 16, 1999, http://www.lubbockonline.com.
28. Ibid.
29. J. C. Chambers, "Outstanding Lubbock Leaders: 1976–Present." *Lubbock Avalanche-Journal*, March 25, 1999, http://www.lubockonline.com.
30. T. J. Patterson interview by Phil Price, August 22, 2008.
31. Reverend Sonia J. Scott interview by Phil Price, March 2, 2009.
32. "Council Renews Juvenile Curfew Ordinance with 7-0 Vote," KCBD, 2013, http://www.kcbd.com.
33. Avis Elise Patterson interview by Phil Price, April 8, 2009.
34. T. J. Patterson, Jr., interview by Phil Price, March 3, 2008.
35. Shelia Patterson Harris interview by Phil Price, April 14, 2009.
36. T. J. Patterson interview by Daniel Sanchez, Texas Tech University Southwest Collection/Special Collections, July 26, 2004.
37. T. J. Patterson and Eddie Richardson interview by Eric Strong, "The History of the *Southwest Digest*," October 1, 2007.
38. Adam D. Young, "Patterson Fundraiser Raises Laughs, Smiles," October 24, 2011, http://www.redraiders.com.
39. Irie Price, "Road to Honor T. J. Patterson, Raise Funds for Charitable Causes," *Lubbock Avalanche-Journal*, October 17, 2011, http://www.lubbockonline.com.
40. "Obituary: Bobbie Gean Patterson," http://www.legacy.com. Adam Young, "T. J. Patterson Wife, Bobbie Patterson, Dies Friday at Age 73," *Lubbock Avalanche-Journal*, January 13, 2012, http://www.lubbockonline.com.
41. Ray Westbrook, "Paterson's [sic] Years of Service in Public Eye Have Made Him a Hero to Many," *Lubbock Avalanche-Journal*, May 16, 1999, http://www.lubbockonline.com.
42. Matt Dotray, "Milestone: Patterson Celebrates 30 Years of Texas Association of Black City Council Members," *Lubbock Avalanche-Journal*, October 18, 2016, http://www.lubbockonline.com.
43. Austin Kemker, "T. J. Patterson Reflects As Daughter Takes Office He Held," July 5, 2016, http://www.oldies977lubbock.com.

Index

Page numbers in *italics* represent photographs.

About the Author

Phil Price has been friends with T. J. Patterson for more than twenty years. Now retired, Price was President and CEO of a marketing and design agency. Over the years he has served the Lubbock Independent School District, the Lubbock Better Business Bureau, the Lubbock Chamber of Commerce, and other city agencies. He lives in Lubbock with his wife, Victoria.